CATHERINE CRIER

CONTEMPT

HOW THE RIGHT IS WRONGING

AMERICAN JUSTICE

RUGGED LAND | 401 WEST STREET · SECOND FLOOR · NEW YORK CITY · NY 10014 · USA

RuggedLand

Published by Rugged Land, LLC

401 WEST STREET • SECOND FLOOR • NEW YORK • NY • 10014 • USA

RUGGED LAND and colophon are trademarks of Rugged Land, LLC.

PUBLISHER'S CATALOGING-IN-PUBLICATION DATA

(Provided by Quality Books, Inc.)

Crier, Catherine.
Contempt : how the right is wronging American justice
/ by Catherine Crier. -- 1st ed.

p. cm.

ISBN 1-59071-064-9

1. Law and politics. 2. Judicial process--United States.
3. Political questions and judicial power--
United States. 4. Conservatism--United States.
I. Title.

K487.P65C75 2005   340'.11
QBI05-700302

RUGGED LAND WEBSITE ADDRESS: WWW.RUGGEDLAND.COM

1   3   5   7   9   10   8   6   4   2

First Edition

"The greatest threat to civility—and ultimately to civilization—is an excess of certitude. The world is much menaced just now by people who think that the world and their duties in it are clear and simple. They are certain that they know what—who—created the Universe and what this creator wants them to do to make our little speck in the Universe perfect, even if extreme measures—even violence—are required.

America is currently awash in an unpleasant surplus of clanging, clashing certitudes. That is why there is a rhetorical bitterness absurdly disproportionate to our real differences. It has been well said that the spirit of Liberty is the spirit of not being too sure that you are right. One way to immunize ourselves against misplaced certitude is to contemplate—even to savor—the unfathomable strangeness of everything, including ourselves."

—GEORGE F. WILL *(2005)*

TABLE OF CONTENTS

TABLE OF CONTENTS

CHAPTER ONE
BE VERY AFRAID

On August 14, 2005, at 7:00 p.m. EDT, the Family Research Council aired a television special watched by an estimated seventy-nine million viewers (twenty-seven million more viewers than watched the last episode of *Friends*). And you may not have even heard of the program—*Justice Sunday II*.

Taped at the Two Rivers Baptist Churchin Nashville, Tennessee, it featured born-again religious leaders, ultraconservative politicians, and right-wing special-interest-group directors. The promotional flyer proclaimed, "How activist judges subvert the family, undermine religious freedom, and threaten our nation's survival." The producers said their show concerned "the absence of evangelical beliefs in our country's judicial branch." Their first installment, *Justice Sunday*, which aired April 24, 2005, had been just as popular.

James Dobson, founder of the fundamentalist religious group Focus on the Family, wasted no time as the broadcast began. America's judges are "unelected, unaccountable, and arrogant," he charged, and "...believe they know better than the American people about the direction the country should go." Michael Donohue, president of the Catholic League, demanded a constitutional amendment that would state that "unless a [Supreme Court] judicial vote is unanimous, you cannot overturn a law created by Congress." The Court, he bellowed, is trying to "take the hearts and soul of our culture."

To hear the *Justice Sunday* people tell it, judges are outlaws and murderers, part of a conspiracy that sabotages people of faith and rejects the sanctity of life. They echo Pat Robertson's sentiment: "These judges actually despise the country and all it stands for; therefore, they believe that the best way to undermine and humiliate America is to break down its laws, morals, beliefs, and standards, and to bring about as much cultural anarchy as possible, so that the nation will eventually destroy itself. "

Though members of this radical faction constitute a minority in America, they wield a great deal of clout. Their influence is disproportionate to their size; but their power comes from their organization, their commitment, and their unshakeable sense of righteousness.

The extreme Right has conquered the executive and legislative branches of government, but it has not been able to bring the federal courts to heel...yet. Undoubtedly, this group has a prodigious impact on the Supreme Court and the other federal courts, but it wants so much more. Its leaders have taken an entity that innately resists politics and turned it into a highly politicized battle zone. They seethe over this unelected, independent third branch of government, the last bulwark between the American people and their attempted coup. That some federal judges have proven well educated, fair, and unintimidated by these voices and methods has further stymied their best-laid plans. The extreme Right may control a good part of the castle, but they have yet to breach the citadel. Only, make no mistake, they mean to bring every last wall crashing down.

And if they manage this, what will they do?

Most of them would like to see the United States under biblical law. Comparable to countries like Sudan, Saudi Arabia, and Iran, all of which live by Sharia (the strict Islamic code of the Koran), America's right-wing fundamentalists seek a nation governed by Old and New Testament scripture. Born-again Christianity will supplant the Constitution. This is no exaggeration—purchase a DVD of either *Justice Sunday* event, buy a book by one of their ministers, or simply go to one of their web sites. They do not make a secret of it. What's more, they demand that all Americans adhere to their rigid and reactionary beliefs.

Some readers may stop reading at this point, unwilling to listen to some "liberal" blast the extreme Right, but I beg your indulgence for a few lines more. I began my career as an assistant district attorney in Dallas County, Texas, and am responsible for criminals serving thousands of years in the Texas Department of Corrections. I was an elected Republican judge in Texas from 1984–1989. Suffice it to say, I was not then, nor am I now, some radical lefty out to denounce every position expressed by the conservatives in this country.

I am, however, a long-time student of the political system in this country, with an obvious focus on our judiciary. I have lectured for years on the importance of the courts and the need for American citizens to understand the role judges play in our government. I wrote the book *The Case Against Lawyers* in 2002. This book castigated behavior on the left and the right of the political spectrum. I raised objections to certain government regulations of business and education, challenged particular restrictions on law enforcement, and pointed out much-needed tort reforms. On the other hand, I criticized the death penalty, sentencing guidelines, environmental abuses, and infringements on personal liberties. One of my favorite book reviews called me a "non-ideological basher" regarding problems in our institutions of government and justice.

Today I consider myself a true independent with some libertarian leanings. Thoughtful conservatives are not the target of my contempt. I have praise as well as criticism of the Rehnquist court. Instead, I am concerned about the activist, reactionary, radical group far to the right of Justice O'Connor, Kennedy, or in many instances, even Rehnquist. And despite my concerted attack on religious fundamentalists and ultraconservatives in these pages, it is not their personal religious beliefs that I challenge; it is their stated intent to foist those beliefs on the rest of us by overthrowing our judicial system and America's constitutional democracy.

Though the debate over judges has only recently come up on the national radar, it has been quite heated in legal and political circles for several decades. An activist judge, or one who "makes law," is frequently called "liberal" and denigrated, while "originalists," or those who "strictly interpret" the Constitution, are usually deemed "conservative" and revered, at least by the very vocal extreme right wing that is putting American justice on trial. But these terms ignorantly pit political ideology against legal realities. As weapons, this rhetoric sounds quite damning, but the words are meaningless.

When opinions are analyzed, judges regularly move from one camp to another regardless of their labels or stated philosophy. "Originalists" have discovered meaning in the Constitution that does not exist, and "activist" judges have exercised considerable restraint when asked to strike down or change our laws. Often, judges render decisions that cannot be explained by their legal philosophy because they are more interested in justice than rigid consistency with a theory of constitutional interpretation. Ultimately, these categories are effective buzzwords used to inflame an uninformed electorate. In recent years, the Far Right has utilized this tactic for one purpose alone: to capture the last somewhat independent branch of our government.

The Far Right wants to control our federal judiciary in order to enact its specific reactionary agenda. At first blush, this agenda would seem to center on social issues—abortion, gay rights, affirmative action, and religion in schools. These items certainly garner the most press attention, but don't be fooled. There is another insidious aspect to their designs. Economic and political issues are crucial to them as well. If they are successful in our federal courts, this plot will have a profound impact on citizens in every arena. They are making efforts to curtail federal regulation of businesses, environmental protections, worker's rights, bankruptcy laws, tort liability, and property interests, among other causes.

This radical group also wants much more control exerted by the states. For over a century, the federal courts have built a safety net in order to uniformly protect the constitutional rights of every American. But as Edwin Meese began arguing in the 1980s that the Bill of Rights does not apply to the states, the extreme Right believes that such Constitutional protections only exist to inhibit action by the national government. They want our individual guarantees surrendered back to the states, where enforcement will diminish and maybe disappear altogether.

Despite the Far Right's claims that they want the courts to leave Congress alone, they actually aim to reduce congressional authority. They want ultraconservative judges to strike down a great deal more federal legislation *and* to negate decades of legal precedent—the very definition of "reactionary." The extreme Right may argue against judicial "activism," but they certainly know how to practice it.

And through it all they camouflage these issues under a shiny veneer of values, morality, and religion.

Should the nation have minimum wage laws? Should corporations be held responsible when they commit serious wrongs? Should our environment, the air and water, be protected from polluters large and small? Should the Bill of Rights apply to all of the states, or should we have fifty different fiefdoms wherein a simple majority of state legislators can decide our fates?

For the first time since the early twentieth century, these items are actually in play.

Of course, the key to each and every one of these issues is the federal courts. And this drives the extreme Right to distraction. They have nothing but disdain for the founding fathers' belief in three branches of government and the prescient system of checks and balances. Indeed, they are rewriting America's revolutionary history to accommodate their point of view.

In the wake of the Terri Schiavo debacle, I wanted to write a book in defense of the federal court system and its judges and to explain how, though imperfect, the system has evolved very much as the founders intended.

But I don't want that anymore. Now I want this book to be a wake-up call, a warning flare, a political stun grenade that provokes the silent majority of this country to stand up and take notice.

When I was campaigning for the 162nd Dallas Court in the spring of 1984, I used to tell voters, "You may never meet your senator or congressman, you many never need these people, but you will need your judge. Whether your child gets in trouble with the law, a business deal goes bad, there is a divorce in the family, or someone dies and a will must be probated, at some point you will likely need our courts. That is not the time to discover the character and quality of the bench." While I was referencing the state courts rather than a federal bench, the argument is the same—but the impact on each citizen is immeasurably greater.

Judge John Roberts has been nominated for our highest court. With apologies to the remaining eight justices, it is likely that President Bush will have the opportunity to promote one or more additional judges to the Supreme Court before his term ends on January 20, 2009. I cannot overemphasize the importance of these appointments to our nation's future.

For all of those Americans who believe that our democracy is safe, you are wrong. Today, the radical Right is winning, and they know it. Sooner rather than later, we may be living in a very different country, a country that had been ours, a country that will be theirs.

THE BILL OF ~~RIGHTS~~ THE RIGHT

Amendments 1-~~10~~ 9 of the Constitution

═══════════════════════════════════════

Amendments I

Congress shall make ~~no~~ _any_ law ~~respecting an~~ _encouraging the_ establishment of _the Christian_ religion, _and shall make no law_ ~~or prohibiting~~ _inconveniencing_ the free exercise thereof; or ~~abridging~~ _promoting_ the freedom of _Christian_ speech~~, or of the press~~; or the right of ~~the people~~ _Christians_ peaceably _or otherwise_ to ~~assemble~~ _protest~~, and to petition the government for a redress of grievances~~._

Amendments II

A ~~well regulated militia~~ _heavily armed population_, being necessary to the security of a free state, the right of the people to ~~keep~~ _buy_ and ~~bear~~ _own_ arms _of any kind and number_, shall not be infringed.

Amendments III

~~No soldier shall, in time of peace be quartered in any house, without the consent of the owner, nor in time of war, but in a manner to be prescribed by law.~~ _In times of undeclared war, the government shall reserve the right to defend the country against its enemies by any means necessary._

Amendments IV

The ~~right~~ _power_ of the ~~people~~ _government_ to ~~be secure in their~~ _search_ persons, houses, papers, and effects, ~~against unreasonable searches and seizures,~~ shall not be ~~violated~~ _restricted_, and ~~no~~ warrants shall issue, but upon ~~probable~~ cause, supported by oath or affirmation, and ~~particularly~~ _generally_ describing the place to be searched, and the persons or things to be seized.

No person shall be held to answer for a capital, or otherwise infamous crime, unless on a presentment or indictment of a grand jury, except in cases arising in the land or naval forces, or in the militia, when in actual service in time of *undeclared* war or public danger; nor shall any person be subject for the same offense to be twice put in jeopardy of life or limb; ~~nor shall be compelled in any criminal case to be a witness against himself~~, nor be deprived of ~~life, liberty, or~~ property, without due process of law; nor shall private property be taken ~~for public use, without just compensation~~.

Amendments VI

In all criminal prosecutions, the accused shall enjoy the right to a ~~speedy and public~~ trial, by ~~an impartial~~ *a* jury of the state and district wherein the crime shall have been committed, which district shall have been previously ascertained by law, and to be informed of the nature and cause of the accusation; to be confronted with the witnesses against him; to have compulsory process for obtaining witnesses in his favor~~, and to have the assistance of counsel for his defense~~.

Amendments VII

In suits at common law, where the value in controversy shall exceed ~~twenty~~ *one million* dollars, the right of trial by jury shall be preserved, and no fact tried by a jury, shall be otherwise reexamined in any court of the United States, than according to the rules of the common law.

Amendments VIII

Excessive bail shall ~~not~~ be required, ~~nor excessive fines~~ *and punitive damages shall not be* imposed~~, nor cruel and unusual punishments inflicted~~.

Amendments IX

~~The enumeration in the Constitution, of certain rights, shall not be construed to deny or disparage others retained by the people.~~

Amendments X

The powers not delegated to the United States by the Constitution, nor prohibited by it to the states, are reserved to the states ~~respectively, or to the people.~~

> **CONTEMPT:** Willful disobedience to or open disrespect of a court, judge, or legislative body.

Many of the terms I use in this book to describe political beliefs may sound extreme. They're not. Unlike the majority of the language used today in politics, these words are accurate.

For instance, some of my friends are "conservatives," "moderates," and "liberals." Depending on the issue at hand, I am often all three. The people intent on taking over America are not. They are reactionaries. If you don't believe me, here are some political definitions from the *Merriam-Webster's Collegiate Dictionary*, Eleventh Edition.

> **CONSERVATIVE:** Tending or disposed to maintain existing views, conditions, or institutions:
>
> **REACTIONARY:** Tending toward a former and usually outmoded political or social order or policy... ultraconservative in politics.
>
> **MODERATE:** Professing or characterized by political or social beliefs that are not extreme.
>
> **LIBERAL:** Open minded or not strict in the observance of orthodox, traditional, or established forms or ways.

Since the religious Right plays a large role in today's politics, it's important to be clear on just who we're talking about.

EVANGELICAL: Emphasizing salvation by faith in the atoning death of Jesus Christ through personal conversion, the authority of Scripture, and the importance of preaching as contrasted with ritual.

BORN-AGAIN: Of, relating to, or being a usually Christian person who has made a renewed or confirmed commitment of faith especially after an intense religious experience.

FUNDAMENTALISM: A movement in 20th century Protestantism emphasizing the literally interpreted Bible as fundamental to Christian life and teaching.

CHAPTER TWO

A TALE OF TWO JUDGES

In letters to the editor, blogs, on the streets, and on TV, they called him a murderer. Worse than Pontius Pilate. "Are you related to Mengele, or just a student?" asked one outraged writer. A legal scholar said he should be prosecuted as a torturer. Congressmen called him a terrorist. A man in North Carolina offered $50,000 to anyone willing to wipe him off the face of the earth.

They were speaking not of Osama bin Laden but of a quiet, unfailingly polite, completely bald sixty-three-year-old Florida judge named George Greer. Greer seems an unlikely target for so much hate. He has led a mostly quiet life. After graduating from Florida State University and the University of Florida Law School, he moved home to Clearwater in the late sixties. He started a law practice, raised twin boys, joined a Baptist church, and attended it regularly. He actively participated in local charities. In 2002 he offered to give a friend who needed a transplant one of his kidneys.

A political and religious conservative ("George *is* the religious right," a friend would later say), Greer ran for and won a seat on the county commission in 1984. Eight years later he gave up the hustle and bustle of politics to become a judge. He believed this was the highest way a lawyer could serve his fellow citizens. Considered thoughtful and deliberate, he particularly understands the plight of the disabled, for Greer is legally blind and cannot drive.

So how did he manage to attract so much venom? Quite simply, he did his job. This is the fate these days of judges who offend the religious Right, even if their only "crime" is upholding the law.

Greer always thought his biggest claim to fame would be the fact that at FSU he lived briefly in the same house with Jim Morrison, the future lead singer of the Doors. (Greer and his roommates kicked the uncontrollable Morrison out after only one semester.) But in 2000, when Terri Schiavo's tragic case came before his court, Greer learned the hard way that living with an unruly future rock star was nothing compared to enduring the threats and intimidation of Christian evangelicals fired with righteous anger.

Greer's story is a lesson in hypocrisy. Everything that evangelical conservatives pretend to care about—judicial restraint, the separation of powers, federalism, the Constitution, even life—was betrayed in the Schiavo case. What is really important to them, the story reveals, is not the Constitution or moral principles, but an extremist agenda to destroy our freedoms. The content of *that* agenda is told in the story of Roy Moore, a judge who had a much different experience from George Greer's.

Terri Schiavo worked at an insurance company. She liked stuffed animals and romance novels. She struggled with her weight as a teenager but resolutely shed pounds as a senior in high school. After marrying her husband Michael at age twenty, she continued to lose weight and may have developed an eating disorder. In the early morning hours of February 25, 1990, Michael heard a thump in the hallway and found his wife unconscious on the floor. Paramedics quickly arrived to treat Terri, but she never regained consciousness. She was twenty-six.

For eight years Michael cared for his wife, seeking experimental treatments and new stimuli—museums, new clothes, tapes of friends and family—to try to bring her back. He even became a nurse to better tend to her. Nothing worked. In 1998, Michael finally filed a petition to discontinue his wife's life support. The case was assigned to George Greer.

The case garnered national attention only because Terri Schiavo's parents, Robert and Mary Schindler, opposed the petition. In the first few years after Terri collapsed, the Schindlers and Michael had gotten along well, but in 1993 they argued over how to split a $700,000 malpractice award in connection with Terri's treatment. By the time Michael filed his petition, he had not spoken to his in-laws in years. The Schindlers fought him, arguing that Terri should be kept alive.

The overwhelming evidence presented to Greer at trial supported the conclusions that Terri was in a persistent vegetative state, that she had no hope of recovery, and that her death would be painless. Terri had the right to refuse medical care for herself, but because she was unconscious, she could not say what she wanted.

In such circumstances, Florida statute and case law (which is similar to the law in thirty other states) allows the termination of a patient's life support if "clear and convincing evidence" establish that is what the patient would have wanted. The issue then, was whether Terri would have wished to be kept on life support.

Michael Schiavo and his relatives testified that Terri had said that she would prefer to die rather than remain in a vegetative state. The Schindlers argued that Terri had made statements contradicting this, but those statements, according to the court record, were either made when Terri was eleven or twelve years old or concerned what she would do for other people, not for herself.

Greer found the Schindlers' evidence unconvincing, and in February 2000 ordered the removal of Terri Schiavo's feeding tube. The Schindlers immediately appealed. The case began to draw notice from right-to-life activists, but for the next few years it simply dragged through the courts.

Roy Moore, meanwhile, struggled with an interior-decoration problem. It was 1992, and Moore had just been appointed a circuit judge in Gadsden, in northeast Alabama. When he inspected his new courtroom, with its low ceiling and "buzzing fluorescent lights," he thought it could use some pictures of presidents to add a "sense of dignity." But, as Moore writes in his autobiography, "Finding portraits of sufficient size and quality for a courtroom was difficult. One day as I was standing in the dining room of my home, the Ten Commandments plaque I had made twelve years before caught my eye...The plaque seemed to be the answer to my quest for something fitting on the wall behind my bench." This effort to fill empty wall space would beget years of litigation, cost millions of dollars, and end in a constitutional crisis.

Moore's appointment to a judgeship represented a huge personal triumph. A West Point graduate and Vietnam veteran with a penchant for writing poetry, he had returned to his home state to practice law. But at age thirty-five he gave up his practice after unsuccessfully battling what he terms the "courthouse crowd" and its way of doing things. After working odd jobs for a while, he left Gadsden for Galveston, Texas, and trained for nine months as a professional kickboxer. He followed this with a journey to the Australian Outback, where he worked for months "mustering beasts" (rounding up cattle) and "rock picking" (gathering rocks from the fields). After an absence of two years, he returned to Gadsden to resume his practice.

His faith had sustained him throughout. In 1980, Moore fashioned his Ten Commandments plaque. He carved two pieces of redwood into tablets and, with a wood-burning set, seared the Word onto their surface. This was the plaque he later hung in his courtroom.

In 1995 the ACLU filed suit to force the plaque's removal, arguing that it violated the First Amendment prohibition against the establishment of religion. The ACLU's stand was not popular. In the following weeks, thousands rallied in Gadsden to show their support for Moore. Governor Fob James, firmly in Moore's camp, vowed that he would never submit to "pigmy-headed, pea-brained, so-called jurists" who dared to order the removal of the commandments display.

When Charles Price, an apparently pea-brained Alabama judge, ignored James's bluster and declared the display unconstitutional, the governor promptly threatened to use the

National Guard to prevent its removal, explaining that if "we don't have a government of laws, we have a government of men." What exactly the "law" was, and why governors qualified as "men" more than judges, he didn't say.

Judge Price received death threats. The Alabama House of Representatives approved a resolution supporting Moore, and in a bit of grandstanding, the U.S. House piled on with a resolution of its own.

The state supreme court had agreed to hear the case, but, perhaps fearing a confrontation with Governor James and the legislature, later dismissed the case on a technicality, effectively allowing the commandments display to remain. Moore had won. Neither the legislative nor the executive branch had openly resisted a court order, but their apparent willingness to do so— over a wall display!—was a dangerous sign.

Despite his victory, the outcome disappointed Judge Moore. To him, the state supreme court had avoided its "duty" to allow the "acknowledgment of God" by public officials. In 2000 the "Ten Commandments judge" took matters into his own hands, running for and winning election as Alabama's chief justice.

He believed, with a curious mixture of humility and arrogance, that "God had allowed me to win for His glory and not my own." Legally, the chief justice acted not only as the head of the state supreme court but also as the lessee of the Alabama Judicial Building in Montgomery. Roy Moore was about to redecorate.

By the fall of 2003, appellate courts had twice rejected the Schindlers' arguments that their daughter should be kept alive, and

both the Florida Supreme Court and the U.S. Supreme Court had
refused to hear the case. Out of desperation, the Schindlers suddenly began alleging that Terri Schiavo's collapse had actually resulted from her husband's abuse. Judge Greer rejected their motions.

No one denied the tragedy of Terri Schiavo's plight or the suffering of her parents, least of all Greer ("It's been an ordeal for him," said a friend). But the law was clear that Terri had the right to die if the evidence supported the conclusion. It did.

Far from creating a new right, Greer had done nothing more than apply the existing law of his state to the facts of the case. Again, every appellate judge who ruled in the matter affirmed him. This is exactly the way members of the Far Right, who rail unceasingly against "activist judges," say courts should work. So far, so good, right?

Wrong. An activist judge, one who would strip Terri Schiavo of her rights, was exactly what evangelical conservatives suddenly wanted! When Greer set the removal of Schiavo's feeding tube for October 15, 2003, protesters contacted Randall Terry of the anti-abortion group Operation Rescue, who quickly orchestrated a campaign to intimidate Greer and the authorities. Terry convinced the Schindlers to release the now-famous videotape of Terri Schiavo that showed her smiling at her mother (an involuntary muscular response according to her doctors). Protesters set up a twenty-four-hour vigil in front of the hospice where Schiavo lived.

At the same time, they bombarded Greer's office with e-mails, more than a few of which contained death threats. Internet sites vilified him. The Schindlers' attorney said that if Terri woke up and called from her hospice, Greer so desperately wanted her blood that he would try to convince her to die.

Greer refused to give in to the intimidation, so the extreme Right turned their attention to the more pliable branches of government. Protesters appeared at Governor Jeb Bush's residence in Tallahassee. An avalanche of e-mails shut down the Florida legislature's Internet server.

Predictably, the legislature caved in to the pressure. The speaker of the Florida House, who was planning a run for the U.S. Senate the following year, introduced a bill giving Governor Bush the discretionary authority to prevent the removal of Schiavo's feeding tube. After the bill passed, Randall Terry promised that protesters would "hold Jeb Bush's feet to the fire relentlessly. " Bush signed the bill into law.

Ultraconservatives had already proven that they wanted an activist judge if it suited their purposes. "Terri's Law" demonstrated their contempt for the very basic constitutional concept of separation of powers. This idea, that power should be split among the three branches of government, protects Americans' freedoms by ensuring that no one branch becomes too powerful. The idea of the separation of powers implies two prohibitions: no branch may encroach on the powers of another, and no branch may delegate its powers to another.

Terri's Law ignored both rules. Giving the Florida governor the authority to overturn the decision of a court that had tried and decided a matter (and, in this case, had been affirmed all the way up the appellate ladder) rendered the judiciary irrelevant. And authorizing the governor to act at his sole discretion in effect gave him the power to make law. The Florida legislature is not allowed to surrender its lawmaking power to the executive, for the obvious reason that doing so is a recipe for tyranny.

A majority of Florida legislators did not seem to care. In fact, many did not understand the separation of powers concept at all. A Republican state senator who voted against the law said he constantly had to explain to his colleagues that there were three branches of government!

Thankfully, the judges of the Florida Supreme Court had paid attention in their sixth-grade social studies classes. The court struck down the attempt to override Terri Schiavo's statutory rights, finding that if Terri's Law were upheld, the " essential core of what the Founding Fathers sought to change from their experience with English rule would be lost, especially their belief that our courts exist precisely to preserve the rights of individuals, even when doing so is contrary to popular will."

It would take much more than the Florida Supreme Court, however, to stop this relentless quest to negate basic constitutional principles. The torrent of threats against Judge Greer continued, and now the Far Right turned its eyes toward Washington.

As Greer struggled with questions of life and death, Roy Moore continued to fret over interior decorating. In the months following Moore's inauguration as chief justice, puzzled supporters wondered why his Ten Commandments plaque did not appear prominently in the judicial building in Montgomery. Was Moore afraid to risk his new position?

They needn't have worried. Moore simply felt his old plaque was not of the "proper size and quality." He wanted something much bigger, and secretly began designing a large monument whose "size, color, texture, and design" would "complement the stately design" of the building's rotunda. He reviewed blueprints of the building and worked with engineers to make sure the floor would support his creation. He ordered special granite from Vermont, which he knew would take months. The first shipment cracked and had to be returned, increasing his impatience.

Finally, on the night of July 31, 2001, Moore and two workers wheeled the 5,200-pound monument into the building's rotunda. Late into the night they worked, Moore sweating in an undershirt and slacks. An evangelical organization videotaped the scene, later selling copies later to raise money for Moore's legal expenses. As most Alabamians slept soundly, Moore, his passions fired from doing the Lord's work, began to recite some of his poetry: "Choosing godless judges, we've thrown reason out the door... you think that God's not angry that this land is a moral slum?"

The next morning, as the red veil hiding the display from view was drawn back, the gathered crowd gazed at the top of the monument, which had been carved to resemble an open book:

I AM THE LORD THY GOD
THOU SHALT HAVE NO OTHER GODS BEFORE ME
THOU SHALT NOT MAKE UNTO THEE ANY GRAVEN IMAGE
THOU SHALT NOT TAKE THE NAME OF THE LORD THY GOD
IN VAIN

And so on. Moore told the crowd it would remind Alabama judges and lawyers that "in order to establish justice, we must invoke the favor and guidance of Almighty God." He added later, "I am the highest legal authority in this state, and I wanted it there. Doesn't it look great?"

Of course, not everyone thought so. On October 30, 2001, three attorneys who disagreed with Moore's religious convictions filed suit in federal court to force its removal. One of the plaintiffs received threatening phone calls: "God will get you."

On the day the trial began, nearly a year later, atheists and clergy faced off on the courthouse steps. The morning session attracted a crowd so large that it spilled over into the next courtroom, so those workers set up monitors for the audience. Polls showed that Alabamians solidly supported Moore.

But do they really understand what he wants? Many people, liberal and conservative, view the Ten Commandments debate as a trivial sideshow, a costly distraction from more significant issues. But Moore's case is instructive because it helps to expose the true goals of extreme evangelicals—and how they hide those goals behind appeals to religious "freedom" and "equality."

Jay Sekulow, the prominent evangelical lawyer and radio personality, said, "It's not in the sense that we're getting everything we want, but we have a strategy…I've got an agenda if you will. I'm utilizing the courts to achieve that goal. You don't go from A to Z. You go from A to C, D to M, and eventually to Z."

"Z," it turns out, is a very scary place indeed. But to get there, evangelicals begin by attacking the Supreme Court's reading of the First Amendment, which prohibits any law "respecting an establishment of religion, or prohibiting the free exercise thereof." Once upon a time, this meant a true wall between publicly funded institutions and religious organizations. The conservative jurists have weakened earlier rulings to now interpret the First

Amendment to mean that government must be strictly neutral when it comes to religion. If Boy Scouts can meet in public schools, so can Bible study groups. If civic organizations can utilize a school building on weekends, so can an entire church.

The easiest and best way for the government to remain neutral, the Court has sensibly said, is to avoid an excessive "entanglement" in matters of religion. But deciding how much "entanglement" is too much is difficult, and different courts have reached different conclusions. Thus Ten Commandments displays *are* allowed, so long as their context is "historical" rather than "religious." States may lend parochial schools books on American colonial history, but not a film on colonial history or the film projector with which to show it. Nativity scenes may be allowed on government property, but not if they are fringed by poinsettias. Even moderates have lamented the confusion of all this; during oral arguments for another Ten Commandments case heard by the Court in March 2005, Justice O'Connor blurted, "It's so hard to draw the line!"

Here the extreme Right makes a reasonable argument: why not quit trying to draw a line altogether? The founders, they say, never meant to separate church and state. In fact, according to Justice Scalia, they meant to encourage religion because "encouragement of religion was the best way to foster morality. " Why should the Supreme Court presume to draw a line that is impossible to draw, if the Constitution doesn't require it? Why not allow religious displays of any kind on public property?

During the appeal of Moore's case, his counsel appeared to take this position. The appeals court interpreted his statements to mean that literally anything religious could be displayed by a government official on government property—a crucifix, a Buddha, verses from the Koran. This is undoubtedly more than most Americans would accept, but the logic still has its appeal— courts would no longer have to make the entanglement inquiry, and no religion would be discriminated against.

But it is all just a smokescreen—something, in Sekulow's words, to get from "A to C." Moore and other evangelical conservatives do not for a moment believe that non-Christian religious displays should be allowed on public property. Moore himself writes in his autobiography that to "acknowledge the false gods of foreign lands is to deny...freedom of conscience." But the Constitution doesn't say that Christianity enjoys special privileges that other religions don't—so how can evangelicals make the argument?

Easy! The First Amendment, you see, forbids any law prohibiting the free exercise of *religion*. And for evangelicals only one true "religion" exists. At trial Moore himself stated that only Christianity meets the definition of a religion for First Amendment purposes, and he repeatedly referred to other creeds as "faiths."

By Moore's logic, then, the state can prohibit non-Christian religious displays on government property, it could also prohibit even the private observance of non-Christian religions—excuse me, "faiths." To evangelicals, this—along with the imposition of the rigid moral regime their brand of Christianity implies—is "Z." It would be a return not to the original intent of the framers, not to 1787, but to the repressive theocracy of Puritan New England—or even the Dark Ages.

This is not paranoid fantasy. Much of Moore's legal crusade was funded by Coral Ridge Ministries in Fort Lauderdale,

Florida. Under D. James Kennedy, Coral Ridge has been linked to a movement known as Christian Reconstructionism, which seeks to place America under "biblical law."

So far, at least, the courts have resisted. In August 2003 federal district court judge Myron Thompson held Moore's Ten Commandments display unconstitutional. Existing precedent would not have allowed any other decision, but evangelicals still saw fit to begin an impeachment drive against Thompson. It went nowhere. Moore appealed the judge's ruling.

The federal court of appeals, in addition to affirming Judge Thompson's decision, rejected another argument of Moore's— that as the highest official of one of Alabama's three branches of government, Moore had no obligation to obey the order of a federal court if he believed the order violated his oath to support the state or federal constitution. Moore interprets both constitutions as if they were founded on the Bible. Thus a federal order that violated his religious beliefs would violate his government oath.

The last people to make this thoroughly discredited argument seriously were Southern governors resisting desegregation. As a Supreme Court decision said, if a state official could nullify federal court orders, then that individual's will, "and not the Constitution of the United States, would be the supreme law of the land…[and] the restrictions of the Federal Constitution upon the exercise of state power would be but impotent phrases."

If only the pesky federal courts were out of the way, in other words, evangelicals in control of the political branches would be free to interpret First Amendment protections as they saw fit—or, possibly right out of existence.

And the disturbing ability of evangelicals to manipulate the other branches of government demonstrated itself throughout the Moore episode. Following the district court's decision against Moore, the Alabama House voted 89-0 to allow the posting of the Ten Commandments in public schools. The U.S. House later voted 260-161 to prohibit federal funds from being used to remove the monument.

After the court of appeals ruled against him, Moore refused to obey the order to remove the monument. In November 2003 a tribunal appointed to oversee the ethics of Alabama judges stripped him of the office of chief justice. At his hearing before the tribunal, he insisted that the First Amendment did not just permit but actually obligated him to publicly acknowledge God in this fashion, no matter what any court told him to do. The First Amendment, of course, says no such thing; again, Moore was confusing it with the first commandment.

If the Moore case shed light on the true nature of the agenda of evangelicals, the Schiavo matter exposed their willingness to further that agenda by completely trampling on the Constitution.

After the Florida Supreme Court declared Terri's Law unconstitutional in September 2004, the Schindlers immediately began filing new motions in Judge Greer's court. Many had a dubious basis at best; a recent speech given by the Pope formed the basis for one. Greer denied them all. On February 25, 2005, five years after he initially ruled on the case, Greer said he would entertain no further motions and scheduled the removal of Terri Schiavo's feeding tube. After still further motions from the Schindlers, the tube was removed for the final time on March 18.

Over the following days, as Schiavo's life faded slowly away, evangelicals attacked on all fronts. Outside the hospice, protesters with megaphones shouted for hours. Pictures of aborted babies adorned vehicles parked on the sidewalk. Media swarmed over the grounds; Senator Rick Santorum contributed to the pandemonium by paying a visit. Reporters interviewed a woman holding a washtub filled with thirty balls of aluminum foil. They represented, she said, the silver pieces Judas received for betraying Jesus.

Governor Jeb Bush, ignoring the decisions of the Florida and federal courts, dispatched a team of agents from the Department of Children & Families to forcibly remove Terri Schiavo from her hospice. The agents backed down when local police said they would resist absent an order from Judge Greer.

Evangelicals turned up the heat on Greer even further. In Tallahassee, the chairman of the Florida House's Judiciary Committee received an electronic petition with more than twenty-eight thousand signatures calling for Greer's impeachment. He said he would consider the matter. A conservative lawyer and author said Greer should be prosecuted for "torturing" Schiavo (despite the statements of numerous doctors that her death would be painless).

Now under round-the-clock protection, the judge had by this time received more than a hundred thousand hate e-mails. Protesters camped outside his home. The pastor of his own church said Greer should leave the congregation unless he chose to "side with the angels." The North Carolina man placed a bounty on his head. And all of this occurred only a month after a man had killed the family of a federal judge in Chicago, and

weeks after a gunman had shot a superior court judge in Atlanta
in his own courtroom. With his poor eyesight, Greer must have
felt especially vulnerable.

Republicans in Congress, ever eager to show off for
their evangelical base, did little to discourage the threatening
atmosphere. Tom DeLay called the removal of the feeding tube
an "act of medical terrorism." House Speaker Dennis Hastert,
Senate majority leader Bill Frist, and House majority leader Tom
DeLay all ventured their own opinions that Terri Schiavo was
conscious. "She laughs, she cries, and she smiles," said Hastert,
who then stoked the rage of the religious Right by condemning
Greer's "death sentence of starvation and dehydration." Democrat
Barney Frank cracked that the caption for statements like these
should be "We're not doctors, we just play them on C-SPAN."

Evangelicals had already revealed their hypocrisy by pleading
for some good old-fashioned judicial activism to keep Schiavo
alive. They had then tried to circumvent the separation of powers
principle. Now they were attacking another supposed sacred cow
of their own agenda—states' rights.

Florida courts had tried and decided the issues in Schiavo's
case many times over. Florida law addressed the circumstances of
the case. Ordinarily the federal government should not intrude in
such a matter—this is, indeed, a touchstone of the conservative
worldview, which sees "big government" as evil.

In fact both Tom DeLay and Terri's father had confronted
this horrible circumstance. After an accident, Tom's comatose
father was removed from life support. "Tom knew—we all
knew," Maxine DeLay said, "his father wouldn't have wanted to

live like that." Mr. Schindler had the same experience. His mother had been ill with pneumonia, and her kidneys were giving out. Suzanne Goldenberg, a reporter for The Guardian interviewed him about this moment. "He had a conversation with the doctors about what decisions needed to be made, and he 'if I put her on a ventilator, does she have a chance of surviving, of coming out of this thing?' And apparently, after discussing with the doctors, he decided his mother did not have a chance of a normal life, and so he decided to cut off the ventilator. It's not in the story, but he also told me that he wanted the decisions about his last moments, you know, if he were to suffer a catastrophic accident, that he would want those decisions to be made by his wife."

No matter. On the day Schiavo's feeding tube was removed, the Senate's Health Committee hit a new low and issued a subpoena requiring Schiavo and her husband to appear before a hearing of the committee in Washington, D.C. Shamelessly, they wanted that poor woman carted into their political circus. Congress does have broad powers of investigation, and Frist made sure everyone knew that obstructing a person called to testify before Congress was a federal crime. But the move was a transparent attempt to buy votes and to bully Greer, who, to his everlasting credit, said that the subpoenas would effectively negate years of rulings by various courts. He refused to give in.

Congress wasn't finished, however. In an emergency session on Sunday, March 20, 2005, it passed a measure authorizing the Schindlers to seek a new trial from a federal court. President Bush actually flew to Washington from his Texas ranch to sign the bill into law early that Monday morning.

into law early that Monday morning.

More than one judge thought Terri's Law II was unconstitutional, but the courts never had to decide this issue. The Schindlers now sought a temporary restraining order to force the reinsertion of the feeding tube pending the new trial under the new law. But the federal district court denied their request, finding that their claims had so little chance of success that the issuance of a restraining order was not justified. DeLay sputtered that the courts were "thumbing their nose" at Congress.

A last flurry of motions, suits, and petitions followed. Various courts rejected all of them. By the time Terri Schiavo finally passed away on March 31, appellate courts had ruled against the Schindlers more than twenty times. Judge Greer's original application of Florida law to the tragic case had been overwhelmingly affirmed.

Throughout the affair, courts had resisted repeated attempts by the Florida legislature, Congress, both Governor and President Bush to violate the Constitution and to deprive Terri Schiavo of her right to die under Florida law. A judge on the Eleventh Circuit Court of Appeals summed it up: "When the fervor of political passions move the executive and the legislative branches to act in ways inimical to basic constitutional principles, it is the duty of the judiciary to intervene."

And if the judiciary is stripped of the power to do so, who will? The extreme Right does not want you to ask the question, because the answer is *no one*.

Roy Moore and his supporters, of course, are just fine with this. Despite his losses in court, Moore's star is on the rise. He recently helped draft the Constitution Restoration Act, which he calls the "most important legislation of our lifetime." This act would strip federal courts of the power to even hear cases involving any acknowledgment of God by public officials. Judges who ignore it would be impeached. Moore's supporters in Congress introduced the bill in 2005.

Polls indicate that Moore has a good chance of becoming Alabama's next governor, and he has become a major speaker on the evangelical lecture circuit, working hard to rouse the religious Right's thirst for vengeance. "The real issue in this country," he tells his audiences, "is not terrorism, it's tyranny. Tyranny is putting ourselves above God, and our federal courts and the U.S. Supreme Court have done exactly that." Moore speaks often at state conventions of the far-right Constitution Party.

As for the Schiavo case, an autopsy confirmed that Terri Schiavo died painlessly of dehydration and that there was no hope for recovery from her persistent vegetative state. One hopes that George Greer, who after his experience with evangelicals must listen to his old roommate's "People Are Strange" with an entirely new perspective .

One also hopes that he did not read the account of a Constitution Party conference held in Washington in April 2005, just after Terri Schiavo passed away. At a panel discussion the lawyer and author Edwin Vieira turned to a curious source for inspiration on how to deal with federal judges: Joseph Stalin. "He had a slogan," said Vieira, "and it worked very well for him whenever he ran into difficulty: no man, no problem."

George Greer, the literal embodiment of blind justice, would never see them coming.

CHAPTER THREE

WHATEVER HAPPENED TO BABY JANE DOE?

In October 1983, a baby girl was born in Port Jefferson, New York, with severe birth defects, including a malformed spinal cord and excess fluid on her brain. Doctors at SUNY Stony Brook Hospital told the girl's parents that without radical surgery, their baby's life expectancy would be just two years—but even with the surgery, although the baby could perhaps live to the age of twenty, she would be severely retarded and permanently bedridden. The parents, stricken with grief, consulted their family, their doctors, and their clergy, and ultimately decided against the surgery.

Under normal circumstances, this would be a story more suitable for a medical book than one about the justice system. But what happened next should shock the conscience of every parent in America.

Just five days after this helpless baby girl was born, a New York lawyer filed a lawsuit in the New York state court system. A. Lawrence Washburn wanted the court to overrule the parents' decision concerning their baby's medical treatment, appoint a legal guardian to make decisions about the baby's welfare, and order the hospital to perform the radical surgery that the parents had refused. The case of "Baby Jane Doe" entered the chambers of justice, and suddenly what had been a private, heartbreaking family matter was an issue that the courts were going to have to decide.

A. Lawrence Washburn was a familiar name in the court system, recognized as a member of the "right-to-life bar," as the *New York Times Magazine* termed it in a 1984 story. Washburn had often been hired by Americans United for Life (AUL). This organization was filled with heavy hitters in the pro-life movement like former surgeon general C. Everett Koop, U.S. Representative Henry Hyde, former chairman of the American Bar Association's medicine and law committee Dennis J. Horan, and Victor G. Rosenblum of Northwestern University Law School. The AUL funded cases like this and hired lawyers like Washburn to do the dirty work.

The mere filing of the case illustrates the vulnerability of our judicial institutions. You may never need your congressman or senator. You may never be affected by any decision the president makes. But you never know when you're going to be at the mercy of a judge.

At first, common sense and decency prevailed. On October 28, 1983—less than three weeks after the baby girl was born— the highest state court in New York, the New York State Court of Appeals, threw out Washburn's lawsuit and upheld the right of parents to make decisions concerning their children's medical care. The court concluded its ruling unambiguously:

There are overtones to this proceeding which we find distressing. Confronted with the anguish of the birth of a child with severe physical disorders, these parents, in consequence of judicial procedures for

which there is no precedent or authority, have been 35
subjected in the last two weeks to litigation through
all three levels of our State's court system. We find no
justification for resort to or entertainment of these
proceedings.

When you put all of the lawyerly shenanigans aside, what the court deemed at stake here was the rights of parents, more like burdens in this case, to make medical decisions for their own children. Unbearable decisions that require Herculean amounts of pain and love, as in the Baby Jane Doe case, should never be left in the hands of third parties.

With that ruling, the case should have been over and the parents left to care for their suffering daughter. But Washburn was a foot soldier in the pro-life-at-any-cost movement, and the entire radical Right rallied behind his lawsuit. Undeterred by the New York court's ruling, Edwin Meese, President Reagan's attorney general, sued the hospital for access to Baby Jane Doe's private medical records. Meese sought to prove that the baby was being discriminated against on the basis of her handicap. (Although opposed to many aspects of "discrimination" litigation, he was certainly on board here.)

The parents refused to consent to the release of their daughter's medical records. Meese, who once told the ABA, "Make no mistake, judicial power is governmental power," took the job as attorney general with the stated desire to move the judiciary in a more conservative direction. If he won the right to control this young girl's medical care, the government could seize a crucial line item on the radical Right agenda—the regulation and control of private citizens' medical decisions. With a Baby Jane Doe victory, Meese could argue all the way to *Roe v. Wade.*

Meese and his subordinates argued that because the hospital received federal funding, the government should be entitled to review every patient's medical records. The argument had substantial legal weight behind it. In the case of *South Dakota v. Dole*, the Supreme Court would later hold that the government can tie federal funds to federal mandates. In *Dole*, for example, Congress refused to fund highway development unless the state imposed a drinking age of twenty-one. The critical element in *South Dakota v. Dole*, however, is in the fact that the case revolved around two governing institutions, the federal government and the state government of South Dakota. It did *not* involve seizing individual liberties in exchange for federal funding.

An individual's medical records could hardly be compared to a drinking age that would apply to an entire state. Again, saner heads prevailed. The federal district and federal appeals courts that heard the case upheld the spirit of the New York State Court of Appeals' ruling on Washburn's suit and turned down Meese's request. They simply refused to allow the government to inject itself into the parent-child or doctor-patient relationship.

The three judges on the appellate panel were split, 2-1. The dissenting judge, who sided with Meese, was hand selected by President Reagan for his life term. His name was Ralph Winter, a professor at Yale Law School, a member of the ultraconservative Federalist Society, and another of the president's activists who believed that governmental power should include control of the judiciary.

Still, there was more in store for the parents of poor Baby Jane Doe. Washburn filed another law suit, this time in New York's federal district court in Albany. After losing in state court, but still funded by the reactionary AUL, he was now pressing the case in federal court. In the criminal context, we call this double jeopardy: you can't be tried for the same crime twice. Once again, whether or not justice would be served depended on a single judge and whether he would let the radical Right influence our judiciary's core values.

Luckily, the case wound up in the courtroom of federal district court judge Roger J. Miner, a Republican, who had served for many years as a district attorney and state court judge before his appointment to the federal bench. Although Judge Miner was a conservative, he did not rule based on his political affiliations. Miner had respect for the law and no patience for a lawyer like Washburn, who was trying to get a second bite at the apple. He not only dismissed the case, he also fined Washburn $500 for filing a frivolous, duplicitous, and harassing law suit.

But still the battle to control private medical decisions raged on. Unhappy with the rulings, and in an attempt to circumvent the court system entirely in future cases, the Reagan administration enacted a policy requiring federally funded hospitals to post notices encouraging staff to report denials of medical treatment to handicapped newborn babies. The administration was looking for other cases that might find more sympathetic judges, who would rule in the government's favor. For three years the notice-posting policy was in effect, until a divided Supreme Court struck it down in 1986.

Washburn continued his crusade, despite the admonition from Judge Miner. In 1989, he learned about the tragic case of a pregnant accident victim who had become comatose. Doctors felt that performing an abortion would increase the woman's chances of survival but needed the consent of the woman's husband—the unborn baby's father. It would be an impossibly hard decision for anyone to make in such unfortunate circumstances, but Washburn did not want to let the husband make that choice. He applied for guardianship of the woman and her unborn fetus to prevent the husband from approving the abortion. Fortunately, once again, the judge threw him out of court.

According to press accounts, Judge Miner was short-listed several times for a Supreme Court appointment. However, the Baby Jane Doe saga would insure that he never got the nod from a conservative administration.

The legal battles that the parents of Baby Jane Doe faced— involving state court, federal court, an appeals process, and eventually a Reagan administration policy that was overturned by the Supreme Court—illustrate both the complexity of our court system and the way that justice really does depend on the man or woman sitting on the bench. One bad judge somewhere along the line, and the parents would have been robbed of their right to direct the treatment of their daughter.

Had that right been put into the hands of a right-wing zealot, the outcome would have been much different.

CHAPTER FOUR
THE REAL REAGAN REVOLUTION

Whenever the federal judiciary comes up in the media, it usually concerns the Supreme Court. The coverage of Sandra Day O'Connor's resignation proved that the highest court in the land is a hot-button topic. What people don't understand is that lower federal courts, the ones that often go unreported on, have more overall impact than the Supreme Court. That's because these courts hear the vast majority of cases, and their decisions, over 90 percent of the time, are final.

Litigants file over sixty thousand appeals per year with the federal circuit courts, resulting in thousands of opinions. The Supreme Court, by contrast, typically decides fewer than one hundred cases per year. As a practical matter, then, appeals court decisions set the precedents that bind the ninety-four United States district courts on most legal issues. For the tens of thousands of people who appeal cases to these courts every year, and for the even greater numbers whose cases are heard only by the district courts, the decisions of these lower court judges matter a great deal.

RELATIVE CASELOADS OF THE THREE LEVELS OF THE FEDERAL JUDICIAL SYSTEM or WHAT'S SO IMPORTANT ABOUT THE SUPREME COURT?

THE UNITED STATES
DISTRICT COURTS
94 courts
663 judges
350,000 cases heard per year

THE UNITED STATES
APPELLATE COURTS
13 circuits
179 judges
63,000 appeals heard per year

THE UNITED STATES
SUPREME COURT
1 court
9 justices
80 cases heard per year
   (out of over 8,000 filed)

*Each gavel represents 5,000 cases heard

The Constitution says that the appointments of federal judges, while made by the president, are subject to the advice and consent of the United States Senate. And for most of the history of this country, although Supreme Court nominations had been motivated in varying degrees by political ideology, lower court appointments were rarely affected. Instead, a president normally appointed judges based on the recommendations of senators from the states where the judges would serve. But all of this changed under President Reagan, as radical extremists grew in influence and desired more control over the judicial system.

A 1988 report, issued by the Reagan Justice Department's Office of Legal Policy and titled *The Constitution in the Year 2000: Choices Ahead in Constitutional Interpretation*, illustrates the thinking going on behind the scenes in the Reagan White House. The report was a 199-page road map that advocated the selection of federal judges as a means of influencing how the courts would interpret the Constitution and shape public policy in the future. "There are few factors that are more critical to determining the course of the Nation, and yet more often overlooked, than the values and philosophies of the men and women who populate the third co-equal branch of the national government—the federal judiciary," the report insisted. Among the policy issues that the president could affect by choosing the right federal judges, the report explained, were abortion, the right to privacy, race discrimination, and school prayer.

Reagan took the report to heart and began the right wing's mission to transform the federal judiciary into an arm of its radical agenda. Reagan turned to assistant counsel to the president Lee Liberman, one of the founders of the Federalist Society (more on this group later), to examine all candidates for federal judgeships for ideological purity.

Under President Clinton, the right wing took its assault on the federal judiciary to the next level. In keeping with tradition, Clinton consulted with Republicans before appointing many of his federal judicial nominees, seeking to reach across the aisle and find candidates amenable to both parties. Despite this, for the first time in the history of the confirmation process, the Republicans blocked many qualified nominees from ever getting on the courts. Using their leverage as the majority party in the Senate, and refusing to even move the nominations out of committee, they denied an unbelievable *sixty-three* nominees even a hearing, let alone a vote.

Even for the judges they did confirm, the Republican majority stretched out the hearings to unprecedented lengths. In the twenty years prior to 1997, the average time from nomination to confirmation was approximately 91 days. But in 1997, this time frame more than doubled, to 192 days—and grew even further in 1998, to 232 days.

The moderate group, Alliance for Justice, found a disturbing trend in the 1997 confirmations: the Republicans disproportionately delayed judicial nominees who were women or minorities. Of the fifteen nominees confirmed in the shortest time, twelve were white men. But of the fifteen judicial nominees whose nominations remained pending for the longest length of time, thirteen were women or minorities.

Senate Republicans did not stop there. Instead they sought to enact new legislation that would ensure Republican control over the nominees themselves. This was in clear violation of the president's right to appoint judges of his choice. Senator Phil Gramm of Texas proposed that Republican senators be allowed to veto nominees from their respective circuits. Senator Slade Gorton of Washington, chair of a Republican task force on judicial nominations, proposed that Clinton be required to obtain advance approval of a nominee from the Republican senators in a particular circuit.

Senator Arlen Specter of Pennsylvania forced the White House to nominate at least one Republican nominee for every three open slots. When Republicans decided one in three wasn't enough, Specter's colleague Senator Rick Santorum blocked all five pending Pennsylvania judicial nominees and blamed the president for the delay: "Clinton is balking over the one Republican that I want, Pittsburgh lawyer Arthur Schwab...The president's holding the hostages, not me."

Senator Gorton insisted he would not "consent to any current or prospective nominations of federal judges from Washington State unless [his] advice [was] sought in a timely manner and... given significant weight. " When the White House balked at this preposterous demand, Gorton blocked all of Clinton's Washington nominees. Eventually the White House caved in to the extortion, just to be able to fill the seats on the bench.

Because Republicans have remained in control of the Senate, Democrats have been unable to use such tactics on President Bush. Instead, every attempt the Democrats have made to stop the packing of the courts with conservative extremists has been met with redoubled opposition.

Of the 229 nominees Bush made during his first term, only 10 were blocked—by threats of filibuster—which makes Bush's approval rate for nominees higher than any president since Reagan. Still, members of the radical Right paint themselves as losers to increase their appeal in the public sphere. They rant that their nominees aren't given a fair chance. Bush himself says all he wants is "an up or down vote" on his nominees, as if this is the way things have always been done. But don't be fooled—they're not the underdogs. Bush's nominees have more of a chance of being confirmed than Clinton's ever did.

Only Bush's nominees threaten to tilt the appellate courts right out of mainstream legal thought. They generally disfavor laws that protect Americans in the public sphere against racial, sexual, and age discrimination. At the same time, these judges would allow greater intrusion by legislatures into Americans' private lives. They would, for example, uphold more restrictions against abortion, homosexuality, and the right to die. They see the separation of church and state as a fiction. Harvard Professor Lawrence Tribe was absolutely right when he pointed out that the power of appointment can far surpass even the power of amendment in reversing the most basic legal precedents and transforming the way the Constitution shapes our lives.

Republican appointees currently control ten of the thirteen appeals courts; the number will likely rise to twelve out of thirteen by 2008. By then, according to the *National Law Journal*, nearly 85 percent of appeals court judges will be Republican appointees. While many of the more conservative jurists are exemplary and possess an appropriate judicial temperment and respect for our nation's laws, some others have used every opportunity to make the law conform to their own radical agenda—such as these recent Bush nominees:

• *William Pryor*, the former attorney general of Alabama who was confirmed to the Eleventh Circuit in 2004, defended the use of "hitching posts"—in which chain-gang convicts are handcuffed to a post in the sun for long periods of time without water—as an example of *reasonable* punishment. He also called the *Roe v. Wade* decision "the worst abomination of constitutional law in history."

• *D. Michael Fisher*, approved for the Third Circuit, doesn't believe abortion should be allowed even in cases of rape or incest. As a point of comparison, only 15 percent of Americans agree with this radical position, according to a CBS News poll of July, 2005.

• *Priscilla Owen* tried to limit a Texas law giving teens the right to get abortions without parental consent, but with court permission, in extreme circumstances. Attorney General Alberto

Gonzales criticized a dissent of Owen's as an "unconscionable act of judicial activism. " Of the Texas lawyers and judges surveyed by the nonpartisan American Bar Association in 2003, 47 percent deemed Owen's performance "poor"—the worst rating of any state justice. Why then was she being nominated for the federal appellate court? Because she was the most reactionary member of a reactionary court. When the Senate approved Owen in a 56-43 vote during May of 2005, the Far Right was thrilled.

Perhaps the most extreme of Bush's appointees is Janice Rogers Brown. Though an African-American, Brown is on the extreme Right. She has compared the New Deal to the Russian Communist Revolution. As a California Supreme Court justice, she heard a case involving Hispanic workers who endured repeated racial slurs by their supervisor. Disagreeing with the other justices on her court and virtually every federal court that has recently considered similar cases, Brown stated that the workers had no cause of action—the supervisor's epithets, according to Brown, were protected by the First Amendment.

But in another case Brown ruled that a corporation could prohibit a former worker from sending e-mails critical of the corporation to its employees. She found (the other California justices disagreed) that the former worker's e-mails trespassed on the corporation's e-mail system. At work, it seems, racial epithets are protected by the First Amendment, but speech critical of the corporation is not.

Once Brown, the daughter of a sharecropper, compared government regulation to *slavery*. Her outrageous claims have not impressed the legal community. As a jurist she was found "unqualified" by the California State Bar Evaluation Committee when nominated for the state supreme court. This was because she was "prone to inserting conservative political views into her appellate opinions." Very vocal and rabidly conservative, she's a perfect radical right candidate. And she's in exactly the "right" place to do their bidding. Brown was nominated, and recently confirmed, for the D.C. Circuit, the second most powerful court in America.

Many of these judges epitomize the very judicial activism that conservatives say they love to hate. They will strike down Congressional legislation and ignore long-standing precedent, not for legitimate legal reasons, but because these acts and cases do not comport with her "values. " Janice Brown said that after studying the nation's early history, "it dawned on me that the problem may not be judicial activism. The problem may be the worldview—amounting to altered political and social consciousness—out of which judges now fashion their judicial decisions. " Translated, judicial activism is acceptable so long as it enforces Judge Brown's particular worldview! Brown at least gets points for honesty—most evangelical conservatives pretend that the only people unprincipled enough to condone judicial activism are "liberals" (read: anyone to the left of these positions).

Regional courts aren't the only target for the Republican Right. Operating under the regional circuits are the district courts. These are the trial courts of the federal judiciary that handle the bulk of federal cases. Six hundred seventy-four judges in ninety-four districts of this system rule on a variety of matters. Unlike appellate rulings that come down from panels of judges, those on the district bench sit alone, with or without juries. This means their decisions are particularly important, considering that each year roughly 70,000 criminal cases and 250,000 civil suits are filed in district courts and fewer than 15 percent of the outcomes are appealed. These courts, then, have the first and often last word in applying federal statutes and rulings of superior state courts.

Bush has filled over 170 vacancies in the district courts, and there are at least 30 more that have yet to be filled. By 2008, judges who subscribe to his hard-line ideology will comprise at least 30 percent of the federal judiciary that has the most contact with the most Americans. By then, Republican-nominated judges will comprise a majority of the district court system.

The Far Right has already begun a foray into state court politics. This area is ripe for exploitation because 86 percent of state judges are elected. These jurists know all too well the pressures that accompany shorter terms achieved through popular vote. According to a March 2004 survey by Justice at Stake, a campaign to keep an independent judiciary, 71 percent of Americans believe that campaign contributions from interest groups have some influence on judges' decisions in the courtroom. The judges agree, with over 60 percent of state judges at all levels believing that "special-interest groups are trying to use the courts to shape public policy to their own ends."

The late California justice Otto Kraus described the pressure of deciding a controversial case while facing reelection. It was like "fighting a crocodile in your bathtub when you go in to shave in the morning. You know it's there and you try not to think about it, but it's hard to think of anything else while you're shaving. "

Justice at Stake issued this warning in its findings: "After the 2000 elections, we sounded the alarm: no state that elects its judges is safe from the corrosive effects of big money and special arm-twisting...business contributions [now] outpace those from the legal community. Interest groups are bringing the culture wars into state court elections by demanding 'positions' on hot-button social issues from state court candidates...If 2000 was a turning point, then 2004 was the tipping point when the threat spread across the country. The fairness and impartiality of the courts that protect our rights is in jeopardy."

This is the fate in store for our federal judicial system if Americans do not turn back the onslaught from the Far Right.

CHAPTER FIVE

THE BATTLEFIELD

To really understand how the radical Right can infiltrate the system and distort justice, it is critical to understand how the court system functions. Our general ignorance of how it all works is what the enemies of fairness play on—if we don't know what the rules of the game are, how can we ever know when someone's breaking them, and how can we ever feel confident enough to speak up?

It all starts with the United States Constitution, the ultimate law of the land. While the Constitution goes into great detail about the executive and legislative branches, it actually says very little about the court system. All it tells us is that there ought to be a Supreme Court, and "such inferior courts as the Congress may from time to time ordain and establish." Federal judges are to be appointed for life, their salaries cannot be reduced once they are sworn in, and federal courts can only hear a limited set of cases. That's it. Our shampoo bottles provide more instruction than that!

Everything else is left to Congress. And as often happens when things are left to Congress, the result has been something of a mess. The first stop in the federal system is the district court.

And although there are fifty states, Congress has sensibly divided the country into ninety-four federal districts.

UNITED STATES DISTRICT COURTS

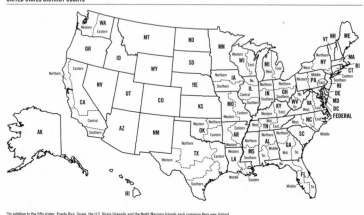

*In addition to the fifty states, Puerto Rico, Guam, the U.S. Virgin Islannds and the North Mariana Islands each comprise their own district.

Some states simply have one district—Connecticut and Rhode Island, for example—but others have been divided into up to four districts. Here's where it starts to get confusing.

In New York, for example:

THE FOUR FEDERAL DISTRICT COURTS OF NEW YORK STATE

Northern

Western

Eastern

Southern

New York City and Long Island, which are at the southern tip of New York State, compose the Eastern District of New York. The area north of the city is (confusingly) called the Southern District of New York. The remainder of the state is split into two parts: the western half is (sensibly) the Western District of New York. The eastern half is (less sensibly) the Northern District of New York.

The lines on the map are jagged, and the sections vary tremendously in size. The Northern District of California is a tiny stripe of land on the West Coast. The Eastern District of California, on the other hand, contains the bulk of what looks like northern California. The Western District of Virginia is distinct from the Southern District of West Virginia, although you could probably be excused for mixing them up.

Populating these courts are 649 active federal district judges, plus a healthy number of "senior status" judges who continue to get their full salaries while taking on a limited number of cases. These active judges handle an average of five hundred cases per year (in 2004, there were roughly 352,000 cases filed in the federal court). Many of these cases never get to trial because the litigants drop the case, the parties settle, or the judge is able to declare a verdict without the need for trial.

Once a decision is reached in the district court, the losing party has the right to appeal. The courts of appeals are divided into twelve regional circuits. As with the district courts, Congress has used its power to create a system that no reasonable person could realistically comprehend.

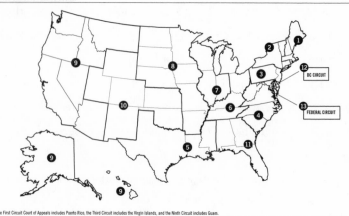

DC CIRCUIT

FEDERAL CIRCUIT

*The First Circuit Court of Appeals includes Puerto Rico, the Third Circuit includes the Virgin Islands, and the Ninth Circuit includes Guam.

For example: South Carolina is in the Fourth Circuit. Its neighbor, Georgia, is in the Eleventh Circuit. Puerto Rico shares a circuit with Maine, New Hampshire, and Massachusetts (clearly, the circuits are not based on weather). The Ninth Circuit is the catchall. It contains the entire Western quarter of the United States—California, Nevada, Arizona, Montana, Idaho, Oregon, and Washington—plus the leftovers: Alaska, Hawaii, the Northern Mariana Islands, and Guam. Not surprisingly, the Ninth Circuit also has more judges than any of the others, twenty-eight. The next largest circuit has just seventeen (the Fifth Circuit—Texas, Louisiana, and Mississippi). The smallest (the First Circuit, with Maine, New Hampshire, Massachusetts, and Puerto Rico) has only six judges. Each circuit's decisions are binding only on its particular district courts—thus, if an appeals court in Massachusetts decides a rule of law, that rule only applies in Massachusetts, Maine, New Hampshire, and Puerto Rico. Other circuits can choose to adopt the same rule, but are not required to. This means that the rules are often different in different circuits.

The District of Columbia has its own circuit, which hears appeals from the federal district court in D.C. as well as from all of the federal government's administrative agencies. Agency cases are often tremendously important, so the judges appointed to the D.C. Circuit are often among the best in the nation. Not surprisingly, a large number of Supreme Court justices come from this pool—Justices Scalia, Ginsburg, and Thomas first served on the D.C. Circuit before joining the high court. President Bush's current nominee for the Supreme Court, Judge John Roberts, currently serves on the D.C. Circuit.

The circuit panel that hears cases normally consists of three randomly chosen jurists. In 2004, there were 63,000 federal appeals, about one-sixth of all of the cases decided by the district courts, and 179 active circuit court judges are assigned to hear the cases.

For most litigants, these courts of appeals are the last stop and their decisions are binding. Although there are 8,000 appeals per year filed with the Supreme Court, the final round in the system, this Court gets to select most of the cases it will hear. During the 2004 term, the Supreme Court accepted only 81 of these appeals—meaning that in the other 7,920 cases (plus the 55,000 that went unappealed), it was the federal appeals court judges who got the final word.

At every level of the federal system, the Constitution demands that the judges serve for life or until retirement (barring impeachment, which is exceedingly rare). The average length of time a federal judge serves on the bench is 25.5 years. The current record belongs to Joseph Woodrough, who served on a federal district bench in Nebraska, and then joined the Eighth Circuit

Court of Appeals. He served for 61 years. Clearly, these judges can leave their mark on the law and on people's lives long after the president who appointed them leaves office.

This explains why the composition of the federal bench is so important, and why the radical Right's actions in recent years are so very dangerous to our democracy.

CHAPTER SIX

THE SUPREMES

The federal district and circuit courts, which are the final arbiters for over 99.97 percent of the federal cases filed each year, are being reshaped by the radical right wing. But at least the Supreme Court is safe, right? At least for the nation's most critical cases, the 0.03 percent that the nine men and women entrusted to sit on the highest court of the land get to decide, the fate of the country is safe, right? It is wishful thinking if you believe the Supreme Court has been immune from the manipulations of extremists. In fact, the Supreme Court is at the center of many battles, and the process has gotten more and more politicized over recent decades.

From its creation in 1789 until Justice O'Connor's recent resignation, a total of 106 men (and 2 women) have served as Supreme Court justices. While the size of the Court has been fixed at nine justices for most of its history, it has been as large as ten and as small as six. Each Supreme Court justice casts one vote, and a simple majority is required to decide each case.

The Court's term begins each year on the first Monday of October and usually concludes by the end of June. During the summer, while the justices normally teach classes or vacation in exotic locations around the world, their law clerks—some of the most talented recent law school graduates in the country—sift through the thousands of appeal requests the Court receives each year.

The chief justice brings a "discuss list" of worthwhile cases to a Friday meeting of his fellow justices. Upon arriving at the conference room, the justices engage in the tradition of shaking each other's hands. Then they sit down at a long conference table to begin their secret deliberations. The chief justice sits at the east end of the table, while the other justices take their places around the table in order of their seniority. Each justice is given a copy of the conference's agenda, and the chief justice then begins the discussion of each case by providing a summary of the case. The senior associate justice speaks next, and then each justice speaks in descending order of seniority.

Once everyone has had an opportunity to speak, the justices decide whether to hear the case—the votes of four of the nine justices are required—before moving on to the next case. After all the cases listed on the agenda have been discussed and voted on, the conference ends and the justices return to their individual office suites, which are referred to as "chambers."

Once the Supreme Court "grants certiorari," or decides to hear a case, the parties will each submit a written brief to the justices setting out their best legal arguments. The Court schedules a one-hour time slot, during which the attorneys for each side will present their arguments to answer the justices' questions. A Supreme Court oral argument is an overwhelming experience for even the most experienced attorney. Although television cameras are not allowed in the courtroom (Justice

Souter has said, "The day you see a camera come into our courtroom it's going to roll over my dead body"), if you were there, this is what you would see:

A few minutes before 10:00 a.m., the court crier and clerk of the Court enter the chamber formally dressed. They station themselves at their desks below the ends of the high bench where the justices will sit. In front of each of the nine justices' chairs are pencils, pens, writing paper, briefs, and a pewter mug filled with water. Four long wooden tables face the bench. Behind the tables sit the attorneys for each side of the case. Placed in front of each chair is a white goose-quill pen—a memento for each attorney.

In the back of the chamber is a gallery for members of the public to watch the proceedings. Because the gallery is only large enough to accommodate a few dozen spectators, people are quickly shuffled in and out to allow as many people as possible to watch. Spectators are prohibited from bringing writing implements, cameras, palm pilots, laptop computers, or any electronic device. Members of the press corps sit in a separate gallery to watch and report on the proceedings.

Upon hearing the sound of a buzzer, the justices assemble in their conference room, just behind the courtroom. In a tradition started by Chief Justice Melville Fuller in the late 1800s, who insisted that "harmony of aims if not views is the Court's guiding principle ," the justices all shake hands with each other. At exactly 10:00 a.m., the court crier bangs his gavel, everyone in the chamber rises, and the crier bellows: "The Honorable, the chief justice and the associate justices of the Supreme Court of the United States!" The nine justices enter through openings in the red curtains behind the bench and assume their seats on black leather chairs. The seating order is set by tradition.

The chief justice sits in the center chair, with the two most senior associate justices sitting next to him and the remaining justices sitting further away from the center of the bench. The crier then continues by saying the words, "Oyez! Oyez! Oyez!" This cryptic greeting is derived from the old Anglo-Norman language, or "law French," which was the language used by English courts . Translated, the words mean, "Hear ye! Hear ye! Hear ye!" The crier continues: "All persons having business before the Honorable, the Supreme Court of the United States, are admonished to draw near and give their attention, for the Court is now sitting. God save the United States and this Honorable Court!" At this point, the gavel is banged once more and the justices and audience take their seats.

The attorney for the litigant who brought the appeal speaks first. Tradition dictates that each attorney begins by saying, "Mr. Chief Justice, and may it please the Court..." But unlike most court proceedings, it is rare that attorneys get very far into their prepared remarks before the justices start asking tough and pointed questions. The rapid-fire interrogation will usually fill the entire hour—thirty minutes per side—as the attorneys desperately try to answer with their most salient points.

After they have heard oral arguments, the justices meet in a conference room on Wednesdays and Fridays to discuss the cases and bring them to a vote. Only the justices are present at these conferences: no secretaries, law clerks, or other potential sources of leaks in a town like Washington, D.C. (where leaking to the press has become an art). The details of what transpires in these conferences are never disclosed. Only recently, with the release of the personal papers of Justices Blackmun and Marshall, have we gotten a bird's-eye view of what goes on at these conferences.

The chief justice discusses the facts of the case before presenting his conclusion. This is repeated from the senior associate justice down to the junior justice, and the chief justice declares the vote. The vote is only tentative, but it does decide the writing of the majority opinion.

The majority opinion is assigned to a justice to write by either the chief justice (if he is voting with the majority) or by the senior associate justice voting in the majority. The assigned author writes a draft with the assistance of his or her law clerks. When the draft opinion is finished, it is circulated to the other members of the Court. The members of the majority provide feedback and editorial comments to the justice who drafted the opinion, while one or more justices in the minority draft and circulate a dissent arguing in favor of the other side.

In close cases, occasionally the unthinkable happens—a dissent is so strong as to convince a justice in the majority to switch sides, and the dissent suddenly becomes the majority.

This process of opinion drafting means that the end result is a product of compromise and contains input from the other justices in the majority and from the dissenting justices, whose views the opinion must deal with. When reading an opinion and trying to reconcile its many lines of reasoning, a reader must remember that the opinion is not the work of one writer but an attempt to accommodate as many views as possible. This is why some opinions grow lengthy and include clauses that read, "Justice *X* delivered the opinion of the Court with respect to Parts I, II, and III, and with respect to all of part IV, except for footnote 6, in which only Justices *A* and *B* join."

From the Campaign Finance Reform/McCain-Feingold Case, McConnell v. Federal Election Commission, 540 U.S. 93 (2003):

STEVENS and O'CONNOR, JJ., delivered the opinion of the Court with respect to BCRA Titles I and II, in which SOUTER, GINSBURG, and BREYER, JJ., joined. REHNQUIST, C. J., delivered the opinion of the Court with respect to BCRA Titles III and IV, in which O'CONNOR, SCALIA, KENNEDY, and SOUTER, JJ., joined, in which STEVENS, GINSBURG, and BREYER, JJ., joined except with respect to BCRA 305, and in which THOMAS, J., joined with respect to BCRA 30 4, 305, 307, 316, 319, and 403(b). BREYER, J., delivered the opinion of the Court with respect to BCRA Title V, in which STEVENS, O'CONNOR, SOUTER, and GINSBURG, JJ., joined. SCALIA, J., filed an opinion concurring with respect to BCRA Titles III and IV, . . .

Throughout this process, virtually all communication among the justices is conducted in writing. It is rare for the justices to communicate on the telephone or in person, even at social functions. The drafting of the opinions goes on completely out of public view. Leaks are extraordinarily rare. The only people who know how the Court will rule, before the decisions are handed down, are the justices themselves and their law clerks.

On the day when an opinion is ready to be released, the justices convene in the Supreme Court chamber and the chief justice announces the ruling. Usually the justice who authored the majority opinion summarizes the "holding." In exceptional instances, a dissenting justice who feels strongly about the result will read a summary of his dissent. Copies of the Court's opinions are released to the public and on the Internet.

I'M HONORED AND ALL, BUT...

Serving on the Supreme Court didn't always hold the prestige it currently enjoys. During the Court's first decade, President Washington had great difficulty getting his nominees to remain on the Court without resigning to accept another position! Justice John Rutledge resigned to become the senior judge of the highest court of South Carolina, his home state.

The Court's first two chief justices—John Jay and Oliver Ellsworth—spent significant periods of their tenure in Europe negotiating treaties on behalf of Presidents Washington and Adams. Chief Justice Jay left the Court when he was elected governor of New York. When his replacement, Chief Justice Ellsworth, resigned in December of 1800, Jay was nominated and confirmed to be chief justice again, without his knowledge, but he declined the nomination. He told President Adams: "I left the bench perfectly convinced that under a system so defective, [the Court] would not . . . acquire the public confidence and respect which, as the last resort of the justice of the nation, it should possess. "

Ellsworth's replacement, John Marshall—who has since become the Court's most famous chief justice—had already twice turned down a presidential invitation to sit on the Court because he didn't want to give up his lucrative Virginia law practice.

Law clerks are a unique institution in our system. Each justice hires four recent graduates from the top law schools in the country to serve them each term. These clerks graduated at the top of their classes from places like Harvard, Yale, and Stanford, and each spent the year before their Supreme Court clerkship serving as a clerk to a federal district or circuit court judge. Just like the lower federal courts are the farm team for future Supreme Court justices, they are also the farm team for future Supreme Court clerks. In fact, some former law clerks have even gone on to become Supreme Court justices themselves.

Chief Justice Rehnquist served as a law clerk to Justice Robert Jackson during the 1950s. After graduating from Harvard Law School, Roberts clerked for Justice Rehnquist. If he is confirmed, it will mark the first time a justice has actually sat on the Supreme Court with a justice he clerked for.

The clerks assist the justices in researching and drafting their opinions, and in the screening process that decides which appeals the Court will hear. Though very young, they hold a great deal of power, especially given the advanced age and deteriorating health of some of the Court's justices.

CHAPTER SEVEN

THE HOT SEAT

For most of the history of the Supreme Court, nominees got a relatively free pass. Very few—only six out of forty-six nominees in the twentieth century—were rejected by the Senate. Today senators probe each nominee in contentious hearings rife with partisan intent. This flies in the face of tradition. The expectation of our earliest Senate was that if a candidate was qualified, he or she should be confirmed.

The first Supreme Court nominee to be rejected by the Senate was John Rutledge. Rutledge had been unanimously confirmed as one of the first six nominees to the Court, but he resigned to sit on South Carolina's highest court. He was then renominated to become chief justice after Justice Jay resigned. About two weeks later, he spoke out against a treaty John Jay had just negotiated on behalf of President Washington, claiming that Jay had been bribed by "British gold," and that "he had rather the President should die than sign that puerile instrument—and that he preferred war to an adoption of it. "

Criticizing a treaty that had just been negotiated by the outgoing chief justice on behalf of the president did not endear Rutledge to Washington's Federalist supporters in the Senate.

By the time the Senate convened for a vote, Rutledge had lost his support and President Washington was, for obvious reasons, uninterested in lobbying on Rutledge's behalf. The Senate rejected Rutledge by a vote of 14-10.

For the next hundred years, politics stayed very much in the background when it came to the Supreme Court. But in 1881, interest groups first began to actively lobby against justices they thought might hurt their interests. The National Grange (a farm lobby) and the Anti-Monopoly League spoke out against the nomination of Stanley Matthews, a former senator with strong ties to railroad interests.

The first public debate over a nominee wasn't until the early twentieth century over President Wilson's nomination of Justice Louis Brandeis. The public outcry was aimed at Brandeis's liberal social activism, but the underlying current was one of anti-Semitism. Brandeis, however, survived the onslaught and was confirmed.

It was not until the middle of the twentieth century that nominees began to regularly appear in front of Congress. When President Franklin Roosevelt nominated Senator Hugo Black to the Court in 1937, it became the first time in a half-century that the Senate held hearings on a nominee who was a fellow senator. Before Black, the tradition had been that senators would be confirmed immediately.

In 1939 the Senate invited Felix Frankfurter—amidst claims that he was too radical, too friendly with President Roosevelt, and perhaps too Jewish—to speak. His testimony lasted ninety minutes. Frankfurter read a prepared statement explaining that he would not discuss his personal views on controversial issues before the Court.

He answered a question from Senator Patrick McCarran about his patriotism by reaffirming his belief in "Americanism."

Since Frankfurter's attendance, every nominee except for Sherman Minton in 1949 has appeared before the Judiciary Committee to answer questions. In 1981, the Senate began to allow radio and television to record the proceedings during the nomination of Justice O'Connor, the first woman to be picked to serve on the Supreme Court. Since O'Connor, hearings have become quite a spectacle, including Anita Hill's testimony, during Clarence Thomas's confirmation hearing in 1991, that he had sexually harassed her.

The politicizing of the Court coincided roughly with the confirmation hearings, back in the 1930s. During the Roosevelt administration, the Court began hearing a number of politically charged cases involving clashes between big business and government regulation. The Court struck down a state law limiting the number of hours a week someone could work, and another mandating that employees be paid a minimum wage. The Court also struck down laws regulating safety in the workplace. President Roosevelt favored these laws designed to protect workers and felt the Court was overstepping its authority. But the five-justice conservative majority continued to declare unconstitutional most of FDR's New Deal legislation, enacted to bring the nation out of the Depression.

Emboldened by a landslide reelection in 1936, FDR tried to break the Court's stranglehold over his legislative reforms by pushing a radical "court packing plan" through the Congress. This plan would have permitted FDR to appoint an additional justice to the Court for each sitting justice on the Court who was over the age of seventy.

Despite FDR's insistence, the plan failed to gain congressional support. His own party would not let him run roughshod over this institution. Nevertheless, because of vacancies during his long tenure, Roosevelt was able to assemble a Court that upheld later New Deal legislation. (Contrary to modern descriptions, this court was "restrained"—it did not strike down congressional legislation— rather than "activist," as it is usually protrayed.)

After Roosevelt, for the next thirty years, presidents (all of whom were Democrats except for Dwight Eisenhower) appointed generally mainstream justices from both parties to the Court. That began to change with the election of President Nixon. Nixon wanted conservatives like Warren Burger and William Rehnquist on his Court. While not every Nixon appointee was what he expected (Lewis Powell became one of the more liberal members of the court, and Harry Blackmun would write the majority opinion in *Roe v. Wade*), the Court began to turn back the civil rights decisions that had been on the books for more than three decades.

Nixon gave his right-wing supporters access to the White House for the first time and paved the way for a true overhaul of the system. The religious conservatives found their champion when Ronald Reagan was elected to the presidency in 1980. Reagan and his administration made a deliberate decision to use the federal judges as a means of enacting a right-wing agenda that would fundamentally change the nation's existing constitutional landscape.

Reagan's picks for the Court—the failed nominees Robert Bork and Douglas Ginsburg, the successful nominations of Antonin Scalia and Anthony Kennedy, and the elevation of William Rehnquist to chief justice—were an attempt to pack the court and transform the judiciary. It is the Reagan legacy—supplemented with President George H.W. Bush's nomination of Clarence Thomas in 1991—that brings us to the judicial era of George W. Bush.

As this book goes to press, it appears that Judge John Roberts will easily win nomination to the Court, replacing Sandra Day O'Connor. Evangelicals have enthusiastically embraced Roberts (with a slight wavering when they learned of his pro bono work on behalf of homosexual rights). Since O'Connor often acted as a swing vote in close decisions, her replacement by Roberts will definitely shift the Court's balance.

But Bush may well get the chance to make one or even two additional appointments to the Court. If a moderate or liberal such as Justice Stevens retires during the president's term, Bush will decisively reshape the Court for many years to come.

Statutes banning the right to die might be upheld by such a Court. The wall separating church and state, which has sparked close and bitter divisions among the current justices, could be torn down. Abortion rights would be curtailed if not eliminated. States might again be permitted to intrude into private acts between consenting adults, and no federal court could intervene to protect them. Federal environmental and employment protections will be diminished, and big business will likely throw off many regulatory controls that, for now, corral their ambitions.

To the radical Right, candidates like Roberts are antidotes to "judicial tyranny." This buzzword became popular in the 1950s after the Warren Court forced schools to desegregate. With Bush nominees in the court, however, the buzzword of the Right might become the law of the land.

AND THE NOMINEES ARE...

Likely Candidates for the Next Supreme Court Vacancy

1. J. HARVIE WILKINSON III   AGE: 60   APPOINTED: 1984
LOCATION: FOURTH CIRCUIT (MD, NC, SC, VA, WV)

Wilkinson began his career with an unsuccessful bid as a Republican for a House of Representatives seat in Virginia. A colleague of archconservative J. Michael Luttig, he was nominated by Ronald Reagan. He later wrote the majority opinion upholding the right of the US to hold Yaser Esam Hamdi (an American citizen captured in Afghanistan) indefinitely without access to an attorney. The Supreme Court later overturned this ruling.

2. EDITH HOLLAN JONES   AGE: 56   APPOINTED: 1985
LOCATION: FIFTH CIRCUIT (LA, MS, TX)

Appointed by Ronald Reagan, Jones called *Roe v Wade* an "exercise of raw judicial power," and also voted to allow the possession of machine guns by private citizens. Considered a potential nominee under George H.W. Bush for the Supreme Court, her ultraconservative ideology and Texas education could make her an appealing nominee for his son.

3. EMILIO GARZA   AGE: 57   APPOINTED: 1991
LOCATION: FIFTH CIRCUIT (LA, MS, TX)

A fervent Catholic, Garza has called *Roe v. Wade* unconstitutional.

Garza is also a former marine, and unafraid to editorialize

in his opinions—as he did in a case involving abortion rights, in which he criticized the Warren Court's right to privacy interpretation. This was a bold move; as an appellate court judge, Garza is required to rule according to Supreme Court precedent, not his own interpretation of it.

4. SAMUEL ALITO JR. AGE: 55 APPOINTED: 1990
LOCATION: THIRD CIRCUIT (DE, NJ, PA, VI)

As a judge on the Third Circuit, Alito has been nicknamed "Scalito" for his consistent conservatism and frequent dissents. A proponent of the archconservative philosophy Constitution in Exile, Alito also dissented in a gun control case and approved allowing private citizens to own machine guns. In his dissent he reasoned that Congress had no right to regulate such activities, an indication of the extremity of his interpretations should he ever find himself on the highest court in the land.

5. J. MICHAEL LUTTIG AGE: 51 APPOINTED: 1991
LOCATION: FOURTH CIRCUIT (MD, NC, SC, VA, WV)

Luttig is young for an appellate court justice, especially considering he has had his post for fourteen years. He has been called a "mini-Scalia" because of his hard-line views as well as his tendency to sarcastically lash out in his opinions. His strict views on crime and punishment could stem from the murder of his father, John Luttig, who was killed in a carjacking in 1994 by Napoleon Beazley. Beazley's execution was put on hold after the Supreme Court—in a rare 3-3 tie—could not come to a decision regarding his fate. Three sitting justices—Antonin Scalia,

Clarence Thomas, and David Souter—recused themselves from the case because of their friendship with Luttig.

6. EDITH BROWN CLEMENT   AGE: 57   APPOINTED: 2001
LOCATION: FIFTH CIRCUIT (LA, MS, TX)

Though she was unanimously confirmed in 2001, Clement has written little in her time on the Fifth Circuit of the Court of Appeals. What she has written, however, suggests an allegiance to the ultraconservative principles of the Constitution in Exile. Clement is also a member of the highly conservative Federalist Society.

7. MICHAEL MCCONNELL   AGE: 57   APPOINTED: 2002
LOCATION: TENTH CIRCUIT (CO, KA, NM, OK, UT, WY)

McConnell has been working to gradually erode the line between church and state since his Supreme Court clerkship in 1981. He has criticized "the enforced secularization of public life," aligning himself with Justices Scalia and Thomas. He also supports a constitutional amendment banning abortion and claims that the practice has lead to a "virtue deficit" in America.

8. JANICE ROGERS BROWN   AGE: 56   APPOINTED: 2005
LOCATION: D.C. CIRCUIT

Brown, an African-American evangelical Christian and the daughter of sharecroppers, is one of the most ultraconservative justices on the appellate court today. Prior to being nominated to the D.C. Circuit she was a justice on the California Supreme Court, even though the State Bar of California deemed her "not qualified" for the post. Her views on federal protections

are some of the most extreme in the federal judiciary; she has
compared federal regulations to slavery and called the Supreme
Court decision in 1937 to uphold FDR's New Deal legislation
"the triumph of our socialist revolution," essentially equating
Roosevelt with Lenin. She was filibustered for two years in the
Senate prior to being confirmed for her spot on the DC Circuit in
June of 2005.

9. PRISCILLA OWEN   AGE: 51   APPOINTED: 2005
LOCATION: FIFTH CIRCUIT (LA, MS, TX)

Nominated to the Fifth Circuit Court of Appeals in 2002,
Owen was rejected by the Senate, then nominated again. After
Democrats filibustered her candidacy, she was narrowly approved
in the "filibuster compromise" that passed some of Bush's most
controversial nominees. In 1994 Karl Rove handpicked Owen
to be a Texas Supreme Court judge, even though she was not a
judge at the time. Alberto Gonzales, the current attorney general,
criticized one of Owen's dissents as an "unconscionable act of
judicial activism" when the two worked together on the Texas
Supreme Court.

CHAPTER EIGHT

FOOLS OF THE COURT

At the corner of Fourteenth Street and Pennsylvania Avenue in Washington, D.C., stands the Willard Intercontinental Hotel. On March 17, 2005, at approximately 8:00 a.m., House majority leader Tom DeLay and Senate majority leader Bill Frist, as well as a number of supporters and Christian lobbyists, met in one of the Willard's sumptuous conference rooms. Although the Willard Hotel is replete with history—Abraham Lincoln stayed there when he first entered Washington in 1861, Martin Luther King Jr. penned his "I Have a Dream" speech there—the men meeting on March 17 weren't concerned with history. In fact, they were there to change it.

At the meeting, Frist and DeLay, as well as two leading evangelical spokesmen, discussed ways to supplant the federal judiciary. They wanted to get rid of judges who didn't subscribe to their ultraconservative views. The stakes were high, so they didn't pull any punches. They wanted judges that disagreed with them *out* of the courts. Disenfranchised, fired, impeached—whatever it took.

One of these evangelical spokesmen, Tony Perkins, president of the Family Research Council (FRC), a fundamentalist

Christian group, put it bluntly. "There's more than one way to skin a cat, and there's more than one way to take a black robe off the bench," he said.

Rev. James Dobson, founder of the FRC, chimed in. "Very few people know this:" he explained, "that the Congress can simply disenfranchise a court...They don't have to fire anybody or impeach them or go through that battle. All they have to do is say the Ninth Circuit doesn't exist anymore, and it's gone."

Tom DeLay thought this was a great idea. Once that was done, as far as he was concerned, the courts "can go meet in Guam."

Dobson explained another strategy—defunding certain courts. "What they're thinking of is not only the fact of just making these courts go away and re-creating them the next day, but also defunding them," he said.

DeLay would brashly proclaim his power in Congress. "We set up the courts. We can unset the courts. We have the power of the purse," he told supporters at a rally later.

Perkins had harsher words regarding unruly judges. The government, he said, should "just take away the bench, all of his staff, and he's just sitting out there with nothing to do."

But certain politicians weren't playing ball. Specifically, Republicans who weren't hard-line enough for Dobson and Perkins. Moderate Republicans who were "squishy" and "weak."

"We need to shake these guys up," Perkins said.

Perkins and Dobson are at the head of the reactionary campaign to hijack the federal judiciary. As their own words from this secret meeting suggest, they'll do anything to achieve their goal. Perkins's far-right lobbying organization hosted the meeting. He once paid former Ku Klux Klansman David Duke over $80,000 for his mailing list—which gives you an idea of the kinds of interests he caters to.

Their list of target judges is long. Somewhere near the top is George W. Greer, of the Sixth Circuit Court in Florida, who refused to overturn a lower court decision concerning Schiavo's right to die. Even though Greer is an evangelical Christian, he wouldn't let his own beliefs supersede judicial principle. That was simply wrongheaded and unacceptable to Perkins and Dobson. Greer needed to go.

The audacity of these lobbyists, intellectuals, and politicians aiming to mold the federal judiciary to their ends knows no bounds. The frightening truth is that events like this secret meeting are commonplace among the cadre of reactionary figures engaged in the fight against American justice. They are well organized, audacious, and intolerant of dissenters in mainstream America. The players are numerous, but the aims aren't. They want reactionary conservative ideologues in the federal court to remake America in their image.

THE HAMMER AND THE SICKO

Following Terri Schiavo's death, House majority leader Tom DeLay issued a statement condemning those who were "responsible," implicating Judge Greer, among others: "The time will come for the men responsible for this to answer for their behavior, but not today." DeLay is a born-again Christian. He believes men and women who don't share his worldview are dammed. When he uses the phrase "answer for their behavior," he's talking about Saint Peter, not even the judges' own consciences. He is saying that the justices who decided against keeping Terri Schiavo alive will burn in hell for all eternity.

DeLay's nickname is "The Hammer," a testament to his political penchant for strong-arming. Ten years ago he was criticized for his brash behavior—now others follow suit. Senator John Cornyn of Texas, elected in 2002, is one of them. (John and I went through "New Judges" school together after our respective elections to the Texas branch in 1984.) Referring to a spate of courthouse violence that occurred in late 2004, Cornyn said, "We have seen some recent episodes of courthouse violence in this country...and I wonder whether there may be some connection. [When] judges are making political decisions yet are unaccountable to the public, then it builds up and builds up and builds up to the point where some people engage in violence. "

Decisions the hard-liners don't like may lead to violence. Judges who rule a certain way might get shot. Then they'll burn in hell for their decisions.

This is not a subtle campaign. According to Dr. Pat Robertson in his book *Courting Disaster*, it is a "battle that amounts to a war of worldviews. The contest has never been harder, and the consequences have never been greater. But this is the challenge we've been given, and we have no choice but to take up our armor and fight. Christ commands it. We can do no less."

WHO'S ON FRIST?

When President Bush nominated John Bolton as UN ambassador, Senator Bill Frist tried his best to get Bolton confirmed. After two failed votes to break cloture—end a debate and get a Senate-wide vote—Frist said the situation had been "exhausted" and no more votes would take place. Only an hour later, after speaking with the White House, he insisted another vote take place.

Frist has publicly stated repeatedly that he is opposed to abortion. Despite this, he retains a large stock holding in his family's hospital chain, Hospital Corporation of America, which performs abortions.

Frist has backed Bush's desire to use only existing stem-cell lines for research since 2001. In July of 2005, however, he abruptly changed his view and endorsed a House plan to expand funding of the research beyond existing lines.

In a conversation with George Stephanopoulos, when asked about the truth in an abstinence-only education claim that sweat and tears could transmit HIV, Frist refused to deny the truth of the claim. "I don't know. You can get the virus in tears and sweat. But in terms of infecting somebody, it would be very hard," he said. This despite the fact that it is medically impossible to do so, something Frist clearly knew.

Another medical faux pas: at the height of the Terri Schiavo controversy, Frist, after merely viewing videotapes provided by Schiavo's parents, insisted that she was not in a persistent vegetative state, despite her own doctor's claims to the contrary. Furthermore, the Schiavo autopsy confirmed her long-standing vegetative status prior to death.

Senator Frist, a physician who makes diagnoses without seeing patients and spreads false information regarding deadly diseases, is not serving his professions nor his country.

CHAPTER NINE

PATH TO THE PROMISED LAND

The religious Right cares not one whit about an independent judiciary, which is evident by the various measures they suggest to bring it to heel—or, literally, to destroy it.

1. TERM LIMITS.

Conservatives generally support making judges more susceptible to political pressure by abolishing lifetime appointments. Many moderates support this idea as well—to a point. Judges, the argument goes, gradually lose touch with the surrounding culture over time, protected as they are with a position from which no one can remove them. Longer life expectancies exacerbate this problem. And because judges are increasingly long-lived, vacancies occur less and less often. Partly as a result, every Supreme Court vacancy now sparks a crisis.

Most moderates, me included, favor term limits if the terms stretch over long periods of time—eighteen or twenty years. Because of the long length, judges would still remain independent of the political process.

Conservatives, meanwhile, advocate shorter limits. Some actually propose such terms should last only six months. "Good" judges would be reappointed—if the party in power approved of the decisions the judge had made. In this way, conservatives argue, judges could be made "accountable."

Moderates, then, support term limits only if the independence of the judiciary is preserved. Conservatives support term limits precisely in order to destroy that independence.

We should resist with vigor the attempt to subject judges to politics. Judges must be free to decide cases impartially, without trying to satisfy political supporters or promoting their own longevity on the bench.

2. JURISDICTION STRIPPING.

Evangelicals have pushed legislation that would strip the federal courts of jurisdiction in areas important to the religious Right's agenda. In 2004, congressmen introduced two such bills in the House of Representatives. They would have stripped the courts of the ability to hear challenges to the federal Defense of Marriage Act or the words "under God" in the Pledge of Allegiance.

Both bills passed the House but stalled in the Senate (which acted, as it should, as a force for moderation). This year members of Congress introduced a measure that would prevent court challenges to any "acknowledgment of God" by public officials (such as the posting of the Ten Commandments in government buildings, or even more critical, any overturning of a legal position based on "God's law" rather than American laws). Judges who ignored the law would be impeached. This bill is outrageous. Congress cannot prevent courts from requiring the

judiciary to base its rulings on the nation's laws and Constitution,
but extremist evangelicals are trying to do just that.

3. IMPEACHMENT.

This is a big favorite. So far, Congress has never removed a federal judge simply because it disagreed with that judge's decisions, but it has been kicking the idea around a lot lately. David Barton, an ultraconservative activist, wrote a booklet in 1996 called *Impeachment! Restraining an Overactive Judiciary*. The book, which circulated on Capitol Hill, encouraged members of Congress to start impeachment proceedings even if they had no chance of succeeding:

> **Even if it seems that an impeachment conviction against a certain official is unlikely, impeachment should nevertheless be pursued. Why? Because just the process of impeachment serves as a deterrent. A judge, even if he knows that he is facing nothing more than a congressional hearing on his conduct, will usually become more restrained in order to avoid adding "fuel to the fire"...**

Barton's "remedy" of impeachment has returned with a vengeance in light of events surrounding Judge Greer and Supreme Court justice Anthony Kennedy, who earned the enmity of reactionaries for an opinion that forbade the execution of juveniles.

On April 9, 2005, at a two-day meeting of the new group the Judeo-Christian Council for Constitutional Restoration, rhetoric went from outrageous to downright terrifying. All the biggies were there. In addition to assorted politicians including Alan Keys, Phyllis Schlafly, and Alabama judge Roy Moore (Tom DeLay was excused to attend the Pope's funeral), there were representatives from groups like the Family Research Council, Concerned Women for America, and the American Conservative Union.

Michael P. Farris, chairman of the Home School Legal Defense Association, told attendees that "Medicare is a bad idea" and "Social Security is a horrible idea when run by the government." In addition to destroying the nation's social safety net, he wanted to end the use of legal precedent by the courts, allow Congress to simply vacate judicial decisions, and, of course, to impeach judges at will. "If about forty of them get impeached," he added, "suddenly a lot of these guys would be retiring."

Lawyer and author of *How to Dethrone the Imperial Judiciary* Edwin Viera told the gathering that when Justice Kennedy acknowledged international opposition to the death penalty for minors, he upheld "Marxist, Leninist," and "satanic principles drawn from foreign law." (Ironically, Viera then invoked his Joseph Stalin line, "No man, no problem.")

House Republicans have proposed a congressional task force to review the decisions of federal courts for evidence of "judicial abuse. " Questionable activities apparently include the exercise of free speech. In April 2003, a *New York Times* piece noted that federal judge James Rosenbaum was the "subject of a judicial witch hunt" because he dared to testify on Capitol Hill against the federal sentencing guidelines that shape penalties in federal criminal cases.

Judge Rosenbaum was in good company—joined by the U.S. Sentencing Commission and supported by countless judges, prosecutors, and defense attorneys. His opinions, however, displeased hard-line Republican Congress members and the U.S. attorney general at the time, John Ashcroft. By simply suggesting changes, Rosenbaum found his own sentencing decisions under investigation and his competency put into question. Some were calling his rulings actually illegal.

Can you say "intimidation"? Such judicial harassment by government officials is atrocious! Maybe members of the right wing should consult one of their gurus, Chief Justice William Rehnquist, who said in his 2004 year-end *Report on the Federal Judiciary*:

Federal judges were severely criticized 50 years ago for their unpopular, some might say, activist decisions in the desegregation cases, but those actions are now an admired chapter in our national history... It is well to remember that [a] judge's judicial actions may not serve as a basis for impeachment.

4. CONGRESSIONAL VETO.

In direct violation of the Constitution, conservatives such as Robert Bork and Mark Levin advocate giving Congress the ability to veto decisions of the "judicial oligarchy." In 2004, Kentucky Republican Ron Lewis introduced a bill in the House that would grant Congress the power to overrule Supreme Court decisions by a two-thirds vote. Congress cannot give itself the veto power without a constitutional amendment, no matter how badly it might want to.

As mentioned above, various ultraconservative groups are aligned behind this effort. These people want their view of the world to be shoved down the nation's throat. If they need to shred the Constitution and over two hundred years of legal precedent to accomplish this, then so be it. Giving Congress a veto over both the executive and judicial branches would—assuming that the dominant party in Congress had enough votes—make the president and judiciary powerless to prevent violations of our fundamental rights by that legislature.

Our founders deemed this concern to be one of the greatest dangers of any democracy. As James Madison said, "If a majority be united by a common interest, the rights of the minority will be insecure. The tyranny of the majority requires safeguards to protect one part of society against the injustice of the other part." His cohort, Calvin Goddard, was more succinct: "Legislatures will in violent times, enact laws manifestly unjust, oppressive and unconstitutional...such laws it is the business of the judges, elevated above the influence of party to control. "

Then again, maybe ultraconservatives *do* get it—after all, imposing limits on fundamental rights is exactly what many of them hope to do!

5. FUNDING.

Congress holds the power of the purse. In March 2005, Perkins attended a meeting with congressional leaders where the idea of cutting funding to the federal judiciary was "prominently" discussed. Three months later, John Hostettler, a Republican congressman from Indiana, introduced a measure to prevent the use of federal funds to enforce the ruling by the Eleventh Circuit Court of Appeals that ordered the removal of a Ten Commandments display from the Alabama Supreme Court building. The measure passed easily with 260 votes.

Sadly, these individuals refuse to examine history. There have been moments when just such tactics have been considered. But cooler heads prevailed, even when this meant opposing one's own party during very dramatic power struggles.

6. ABOLITION.

Congress has the power to create and abolish any federal court other than the Supreme Court. "Very few people know this," James Dobson has said, "that the Congress can simply disenfranchise a court…They don't have to fire anybody or impeach them or go through that battle. All they have to do is say the Ninth Circuit doesn't exist anymore, and it's gone."

So if they can't intimidate the courts into doing what they want, just get rid of them altogether! Abolishing the federal courts would make a mockery of the Constitution's purpose—to "establish justice"—by depriving Americans of a place to seek it.

THE FAR RIGHT WISH LIST

THE ISSUE	WHERE IT STANDS NOW
ABORTION	Under *Roe v. Wade* legal in every state.
CHURCH AND STATE	Separate—no prayer in public school, no posting of Ten Commandments in courthouses or schools.
GOVERNMENT REGULATION	From schools to the stock market, the federal government has oversight of many institutions to monitor corruption, pollution, and fraud.
GAY MARRIAGE	Only one state—Massachusetts—legally weds gay couples, but it is not forbidden by federal law. Eleven states amended their constitutions in 2004 to only recognize marriage between men and women.

WHAT THE RIGHT WANTS

Illegal in every circumstance including rape and incest, maybe allowed to save the mother's life.

Combined—mandatory prayer in public schools, public posting of the Ten Commandments. Constitutional Restoration Act would enforce "acknowledgement of God as the sovereign source of law, liberty, government."

Nix 'em. Constitution in Exile movement calls for pre-New Deal days, including no Dept. of Education, EPA, or SEC. Robber barons delight.

A constitutional amendment stating that marriage is only between one man and one women, thus taking the issue out of the hands of the states.

CHAPTER TEN

THE FOUR HORSEMEN OF THE APOCALYPSE

Although the hard Right's campaign to overrun the federal judiciary is extensive, its most powerful force is none other than a small group of men—the Four Horsemen. So described in a *Wall Street Journal* article detailing their levels of influence, these four—C. Boyden Gray, Leonard A. Leo, Edwin Meese, and Jay Sekulow—combine their areas of expertise to ensure the appointment of judges who follow a hard-line conservative ideology. The Four Horsemen have significant influence in religion, big business, intellectual credibility, and political reach.

HORSEMAN #1—BIG BUSINESS

The story behind C. Boyden Gray is a classic tale of Washington connections. Gray, who helped assure Clarence Thomas's confirmation, founded the Committee for Justice with the help of Karl Rove in 2002; the organization was initially funded with $250,000 raised by George H.W. Bush at a cocktail party in his Houston home. (Gray, incidentally, is George H.W. Bush's former White House counsel.) The goal of the Committee for Justice is to convince big business interests that they, too, have a stake in judicial nominees.

Gray cites the case *Geier v. American Honda Motor Co.* as evidence. The case, which was decided in a 5-4 split in the Supreme Court in 2000, favored Honda's claim that it had no obligation to pay Alexis Geier compensation for injuries she sustained during an accident due to lack of an airbag. Though federal regulations didn't require automakers to install airbags at the time, Geier argued they should have nonetheless. The Supreme Court disagreed, and Honda was spared a costly and public settlement—by one vote. Had one of the five majority justices been replaced, even by someone as conservative as Clarence Thomas, who actually sided with Geier, Honda would have lost. Cases like *Geier* prove Gray's point—that corporate America should keep an eye on Bush's potential court appointments.

Big business believes Gray because he's the moneyman—an heir to the Reynolds tobacco fortune and a businessman himself. A profile of him in 1997 stated that "so many different money trails lead to, by and through Gray it is bewildering." He was the top individual contributor of soft money to the Republican Party in 1995, donating over $140,000 of his personal cash. He also donated nearly $60,000 in hard money to a four-page list of Republican candidates that same year. Not only does he contribute, he gets others to as well. In the same year he forked over nearly a quarter of a million of his own dollars to Republicans, he held a fundraiser at his lavish Georgetown home featuring Newt Gingrich that raised over a million dollars for Republican causes.

His cash connections don't end there. In keeping with the archconservative tradition of backing big business over the little guy, Gray coordinated the Air Quality Standards Coalition in the mid-1990s. The AQSC, as its name *doesn't* suggest, was a consortium of over five hundred companies like Texaco and Chevron formed to fight the EPA's new air quality standards. The standards were adopted after a study showed that when a steel plant in Provo, Utah, was shut down for two years the number of preschoolers hospitalized with asthma dropped by over 60 percent. (Gray was a lobbyist for the company that owned the plant, Geneva Steel.)

Never mind those preschoolers—big business didn't want regulations, and Gray was the soft-spoken southerner on their side. Though he positions himself as an average guy—"I am just a private citizen, a little guy involved in the debate," he has said—he is anything but. His pockets are deep, and the pockets of his associates deeper still. As a Horseman, it's Gray's job to make sure the ultraconservative machine he's fighting for always has the financial grease it needs.

HORSEMAN #2—INTELLECTUAL CREDIBILITY

Leonard A. Leo is the intellectual piece of the puzzle. The executive vice president of the Federalist Society, a conservative organization that vets Supreme Court nominees for their ultraconservative views and intellectual rigor, Leo helped George W. Bush win 52 percent of the Catholic vote in 2004 and was subsequently tapped to head Catholic outreach for the Republican National Committee. The Federalist Society, initially a small organization with little political clout, now boasts over thirty-five thousand members, all lawyers or law students, including Supreme Court justices Scalia and Thomas. Although he has denied membership, Supreme Court nominee John Roberts was listed on one of the society's steering committees.

The Federalist Society has distinct views about the judiciary, views far outside the American mainstream. It has an annual budget of $5.5 million, funded mainly by hard-line reactionary philanthropists like John Olin and Sarah Scaife, mother of Richard Mellon Scaife, the man who single-handedly took down the Clintons. The Federalist Society has massive membership clout and enjoys considerable face time with ultraconservative political luminaries. Dick Cheney gave an address to its more prominent members in the immediate wake of September 11, 2001, invoking the terrorist specter as a way of getting Bush's controversial judicial nominees appointed.

John Ashcroft is, of course, also a member of the Federalist Society. In addition to his morning prayer meetings with President Bush—which although not "mandatory," were attended by many of his employees—Ashcroft would anoint himself with "holy oil" before important functions (his preferred brand is Crisco).

The Federalist Society espouses the doctrine of Constitution in Exile, the basic tenets of which seek a pre-New Deal, nonregulatory America. The phrase suggests a die-hard philosophy, which it is. In short, it aims to strike down any legislation that doesn't specifically appear in the Constitution. Its enemy is Roosevelt's New Deal, which Constitution in Exile's followers would reverse outright. The year 1937 was the beginning of the end, in their view, when the federal government began to create a social safety net and regulate matters like pollution and public schools.

An America under Constitution in Exile is a frightening

prospect. It's a world in which local jurisdictions can make their own segregation laws, can say yes or no to a woman's right to choose, and can allow ex-convicts to buy guns without background checks; a world without minimum wage laws, child labor restrictions, or pollution regulations. These are a few examples of issues federal courts have traditionally upheld to protect average Americans. Constitution in Exile would get rid of them all.

Behind the scenes of this movement are various think tanks and policy institutions. They are frank about their aims, and not apt to shy away from admitting their distaste for Roosevelt's legacy. Michael Greve, of the American Enterprise Institute, explains, "I think what is really needed here is a fundamental intellectual assault on the entire New Deal edifice...[W]e want to withdraw judicial support for the entire modern welfare state." What this would mean, in practice, is an end to federal protections that cannot be found in the Constitution—vitually all protections, in fact.

That's music to the reactionary Right's ears. Business executives like Kenneth Lay, ex-CEO of Enron, wouldn't mind a world like that. Neither would Bernard Ebbers, recently convicted for fraud that brought the multibillion-dollar WorldCom to its knees. In a Constitution in Exile world, it would be very difficult, if not impossible, for these men to be brought to justice for bankrupting thousands of employees and investors.

Those investors and employees have traditionally been protected by the constitutional interpretations of federal judges. That's what makes the federal judiciary so important—it's designed for all Americans, including the little guy. Justices who reject the Constitution in Exile agenda are, in turn, protecting average Americans. But Leonard Leo wants to get rid of these judges and the protections they uphold. The Federalist Society is the intellectual resource he can count on to bolster his ultraconservative arguments. And he has all its power behind him whenever he and his Horsemen meet.

HORSEMAN #3—POLITICAL REACH

Edwin Meese was attorney general under Ronald Reagan. Although Meese left the administration under a cloud of controversy—he was subject to investigations by the United States Office of the Independent Counsel on two occasions—he is still a major political personality. His numerous contacts from the Reagan administration ensure that his three colleagues always have someone to listen to their objectives. He's the man with the connections, with a Rolodex as thick as a lobbyist's wallet. When Meese talks, people listen, and he blazes the trails on which his Horsemen will ride.

"He is our utility outfielder," says Leonard Leo of Meese. "He deals with whatever issue is on our plate at a given moment. " Meese has been a major factor in the Republican fight against the filibuster, and a *New York Times* profile on August 16, 2005 described him as "lionized by conservatives for his role in reshaping the judiciary."

Meese's views concerning the federal judiciary are extreme. Much of the hard-line language the reactionary Right uses today stems from Meese himself, who began his own war against the third branch of government in the 1980s under Reagan. He loves to cite "activist judges"—the worthless phrase ultraconservatives use to attack "unacceptable" judges—to bolster his fellow-archconservatives' position. "The American People," he said in 1997, "will never be able to regain democratic self-government... until we curb activist judges." The curbing is up to his fellow Horsemen, who lobby politicians to impeach judges they don't like. But the language is his, and so is the intellectual showboating.

Nowhere is this behavior clearer than in Meese's advocacy of "original intent," the kissin' cousin of pure "originalism." This term, as it sounds, means that judges should interpret the Constitution according to the "original intent" of the founding fathers. Although such intent is open to interpretation, having been debated by the best legal minds in the country for over two centuries, ultraconservatives like Meese find answers in the most radically conservative readings of the document, and at times clearly deny the specific words and meaning of the founders themselves. The meaningless phrase "original intent" is just another tool to remake the courts to a radically conservative end. Judge John Roberts has been known to have attended his lectures on the topic.

Meese is the political arm of the Horsemen. With his credibility as a former cabinet member, he wields his arsenal of experience, both legally and politically, to ensure his fellow riders their political capital.

Meese is also a fellow at the Heritage Foundation, an archconservative think tank founded in 1973 with money from Joseph Coors, the beer magnate. Meese's position there isn't surprising—as attorney general he wrote a letter to the president of Heritage, ensuring him that the administration would "cooperate fully with your efforts" in advocating ultraconservative policy. In other words, the White House promised to *promote the agenda* of an ultraconservative, unelected think tank! And a rich one, too; in 2004 it received $29.7 million in corporate and private donations, mostly from wealthy, rabidly conservative philanthropists like Coors and Richard Mellon Scaife. Meese brings their money and ideas to the table with his fellow Horsemen.

Members of the Heritage Foundation have written extensively on subjects Meese knows well—"activist judges," "original intent"—to bolster the arguments of archconservatives intent on taking over the courts. If Leonard Leo is the intellectual brains, Meese is the intellectual brawn—he gathers the precedent upon which Leo's archconservative arguments can stand.

HORSEMAN #4—RELIGION

The Four Horsemen represent four different arms of hard-line ideology, and in our modern, hyperreligious age, Jay Sekulow represents the Bible Belt. Sekulow converted to Christianity from Judaism in college. An accomplished attorney , after briefly serving as an attorney for Jews for Jesus, Sekulow became the chief legal counsel for Pat Robertson's American Center for Law and Justice. The ACLJ, as its acronym suggests, was founded as a counterweight to the American Civil Liberties Union, a group considered by many hard-line conservatives to be a hotbed of liberal godlessness. The ACLJ has a hundred employees, including thirty-five full-time attorneys and five lobbyists, and four offices internationally. Though the group was founded only a decade and 01

a half ago, it now boasts 700,000 members and an annual budget of $30 million. The ACLU, by contrast, founded in 1920, has only 400,000 members and an annual budget of $14 million.

Sekulow's job is to marshal the troops—the millions of evangelical Christians who put Bush in the White House twice. But it's a tricky job, because he needs to use their strength without jeopardizing his own credibility on the inside. If church newsletters and petitions are sent out with the ultra-Right's real goal plainly stated—make America a Christian nation any way, any how—Republicans from more moderate districts will get skittish. They don't want their constituents thinking they pander to religious extremists.

Which is where Sekulow's media blitz comes in. Not only does he have a radio show, he has a million-member-plus e-mail list and a national television program, too. His live daily radio show, broadcast to 550 stations nationwide and appropriately titled *Jay Sekulow Live!*, is a half-hour call-in program that deals exclusively with issues relating to the federal judiciary. The show, which airs at noon Monday through Friday, is broadcast from a basement across the street from the Supreme Court. Sekulow also reiterates his views on his television show *ACLJ This Week*, which airs weekly on the Trinity Broadcasting Network.

In addition to being heard by millions of average Americans, Sekulow also has the ears of prominent politicians and judges. Twice named one of the hundred most powerful lawyers in the United States, Sekulow is not some partisan hack—he's an articulate, well-educated spokesman for the religious Right. He's so familiar with the nine justices on the Supreme Court that when he argues cases before them, which he has done on numerous occasions, he can pierce the stuffy atmosphere with jokes that make them laugh, including those that poke fun at Chief Justice Rehnquist's difficulties hearing.

Sekulow isn't joking about the federal judiciary, though. When the filibuster controversy was reaching its climax in May of 2005, Sekulow walked to the Capitol and personally told Republican senator Sam Brownback—his friend for years—to browbeat his colleagues into forcing the disputed judges through. He also contacted Judiciary chairman Arlen Specter to advance ultraconservative judge William Pryor to a floor vote. To not include Pryor on the appellate court, Sekulow said, would be "really bad" for "our people. "

His people, of course, are the men and women who put Specter and Brownback in office to begin with—and they know it. After Sekulow met with senators he used the ACLJ's massive telephone directory to contact 852,000 born-again Christians, urging them to call their senators themselves. "Shut the Senate phones down," he said.

THE CONFERENCE CALL

Every Monday morning the Horsemen set up a conference call to discuss ways of furthering their hard-line agenda. The call includes White House staffers and other conservative leaders. Although it isn't *exactly* a telephonic version of the secret meeting at the Willard Hotel, it's still private, and packed with insiders. Tim Goeglein, Bush's deputy director of the Office of

Public Liason and a close friend of Karl Rove, is almost always on the line.

In preparation for the call, junior aides to the insiders secure a connection, while their bosses deal with other matters. Once on the line, the Horsemen exchange idle banter. This continues until everyone is secured on the line, the most important people arriving last. Occasionally, even the men in their corner offices in the Beltway of Washington will hear a crackle and a sputter as another honcho gets on. Sometimes it is Karl Rove himself, making time for the call while on the road, or even from Air Force One.

These men, with a host of other ultraconservative peers, are planning and strategizing, *every single week*, in the long war to overwhelm the federal judiciary with ultraconservative judges. The Horsemen initiate the call, and discuss policy and political objectives with a number of others—giving orders, asking for information. It's a give-and-take of power and influence.

The call opens with the news—what has changed in the seven days since they last chatted? How have the battle lines been redrawn?

Where's the vote on our judge?

Is [Democratic Senator Patrick] Leahy still refusing to budge?

Let's e-mail all his constituents and tell them to flood him with calls. Force him to change his mind.

What these Four Horsemen have, in abundance, is experience, networks, and clout. Taken together, they represent every side of the ultraconservative battle for the federal judiciary—big business, intellectual rigor, political reach, and religion. And, as each man's individual credentials would suggest, they wield enormous influence.

The Four Horsemen lead the extreme Right's campaign. But in order for them to be effective, in order for their existence to have meaning, they need the cavalry. That cavalry, as Sekulow's media presence attests, is the religious Right. They are the willing followers, ready and eager to charge the ramparts to create a Christian America.

The Four Horsemen are an aptly named group of leaders. For their followers truly believe in their namesake—the Four Horsemen of the Apocalypse, the four riders who will usher in the end of the world and the last coming of Christ. To the followers, these judicial appointments aren't just a matter of politics as usual.

They're a matter of life or death.

ROBERT BORK: SORE LOSER

Robert Bork, whose nomination to the Supreme Court in 1987 was famously rejected, is still active in promoting his ultraconservative agenda on the federal judiciary. A longtime member of the Federalist Society, Bork was denied a spot on the high court precisely because of the extreme nature of his views. During his confirmation hearings, a senator called Robert Bork's America "a land in which women would be forced into back-alley abortions, blacks would sit at segregated lunch counters, rogue police could break down citizens' doors in midnight raids, children could not be taught about evolution. "

Since being denied a spot on the Supreme Court, Bork has engaged in an all-out war with the judiciary. "We are increasingly governed not by law or elected representatives but by an unelected, unrepresentative, unaccountable committee of lawyers applying no will but their own," he has said, in one of his numerous sound bites excoriating the current court system for not including him in its ranks. Bork is mad that he can't impose *his* will on America.

CHAPTER ELEVEN

THE POWER OF THE PULPIT

Barton Warren Stone, pastor at the Cane Ridge Presbyterian Church in Kentucky, had a vision. The year was 1801. Stone, a solemn twenty-nine-year-old with light, curly hair who had heard of the successes of various revival movements in nearby counties, was eager to create one of his own. He had arrived five years earlier, at the edge of civilized America, to preach and create a Christian community. But it wasn't until he heard about the thousands flocking to neighboring Concord, Lexington, and Indian Creek that he recognized the power of revival. He envisioned people of every age and race gathering together in the service of God. He circulated news throughout various Methodist and Presbyterian meetings that the meeting at Cane Ridge was to be "one of the greatest meetings of its kind ever known. "

It was. From Friday until Wednesday of the first week of August, between twenty and thirty thousand people arrived in the woods surrounding Cane Ridge. Ministers preached nonstop, while rapt congregants, lit at night by thousands of candles in trees and tents, became overwhelmed with religious passion. They fell to the ground, cried out, sang and wept. Witnesses spoke of hundreds who writhed on the ground and spoke in tongues. Others lay prostrate and remained motionless for hours, sometimes for whole days at a time. Group worship lasted until provisions for humans and horses ran out, at which point excited participants retuned to their hometowns to speak of the exhilarating experience they had taken part in.

It was Woodstock—168 years before the real thing. Instead of Hendrix, they had preachers. Instead of LSD, they had the intoxicating power of the Lord.

The Cane Ridge Revival, as it would come to be known, was one of the largest and most influential gatherings of the Second Great Awakening, the religious movement that swept America during the early nineteenth century. From it was born the Restoration movement, founded by Stone himself, which sought to revitalize the Christian church based on the New Testament alone, without the historical influence of Catholicism and earlier Protestant sects. The modern Protestant evangelical movement descends directly from the Cane Ridge Revival. Today, various religious leaders march and congregate the masses just as Barton Stone did 204 years ago.

Evangelism is not new—it has been around since the Apostle Paul. All it means is the preaching of Christian gospel, with the specific aim of saving the souls of the unconverted. Most modern evangelical denominations originate from Stone's Restoration movement and hold that if you believe that Jesus is your savior, you go to heaven. If not, you don't. In 2005, a Harris poll found that 33 percent of Americans defined themselves as born-again Christians. That's a minority, but admittedly a significant minority. Evangelicals can be white or black, blue- or white-collar, rich or poor. It doesn't matter who they are, so long as they believe in Jesus. Although many forms of evangelism exist in the United States, with differing views on church ritual, the sole belief in Jesus as the saver of souls ties them all together. And it all ties back to Barton Stone.

Cane Ridge was not a one-time affair. In fact, similar gatherings occur in different forms every Sunday across America, for we now live in the era of the megachurch (a church with over two thousand congregants). Most megachurches exist in suburbs and have large, informal services with televised sermons and modern music. It's Cane Ridge with twenty-first-century packaging.

MEMBERSHIP ORIENTATION OF PROTESTANT MEGACHURCHES* IN THE UNITED STATES

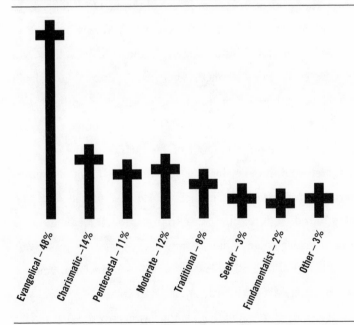

Evangelical – 48% | Charismatic – 14% | Pentecostal – 11% | Moderate – 12% | Traditional – 8% | Seeker – 3% | Fundamentalist – 2% | Other – 3%

*A megachurch is defined as any church where the average number of congregants is over 2,000. (The average number of congregants in a normal, non-megachurch is approximately 150.)

Charismatic evangelists, many of whom spread their message through daily television and radio broadcasts, have been around for years. Although many preach gentle sermons intent on converting the unconverted—steering clear of vitriolic language or political harangues—some of those more established ministers, who preach to a more conservative audience, are unafraid to use incendiary language. And, more disturbingly, their claims are geared toward political rather than spiritual ends. Speaking in tongues in pursuit of holiness is one thing. But telling congregants that your political message is God's will is another.

Of course, this lying isn't always obvious. Many on the religious Right coat their political messages in soft spiritual truths. One of them is Dr. D. James Kennedy, of Coral Ridge Presbyterian Church in Ft. Lauderdale, Florida. Dr. Kennedy has ten thousand congregants and broadcasts his weekly sermons to over forty thousand cities and towns in the U.S. as well as over two hundred nations. Kennedy isn't just a pastor—he's also a reactionary ideologue. And he's not only concerned with spiritual salvation; he's also very interested in the federal judiciary.

Although the primary goal of his church is to save souls through spreading belief in Jesus Christ, it also aims to return American society to "the biblical worldview of the founding fathers," and restore our "Christian nation." Kennedy is a powerful leader commanding a movement that aims to subvert the Constitution to biblical law. "Our job is to reclaim America for Christ, whatever the cost," Kennedy explains. At a rally at Coral Ridge he elaborated to an enthusiastic crowd: "As the vice regents of God, we are to exercise godly dominion and influence over our neighborhoods, our schools, our government, our literature and arts, our sports arenas, our entertainment media, our news media, our scientific endeavors—in short, over every aspect and institution of human society." His proclamations are always met with thunderous applause.

Kennedy's Center for Christian Statesmanship also boasts its commitment to working daily to influence the decisions of thousands of staffers on Capitol Hill. "Our mission is clear," states its website. "IF WE LOBBY FOR ANYTHING, IT'S THE CROSS OF CHRIST" (capitals theirs).

Kennedy, with his influence and political goals, is not unique. With his broad smile and grandfatherly graying hair, he's the very picture of an old-time preacher. But he's just one in a cabal of powerful men, men who are often on that weekly telephone call with the Four Horsemen, in order to convert America "back" to a "Christian nation." Though this fabled nation never existed, that won't stop Kennedy from convincing his thousands of listeners it did.

Another charismatic evangelist who is often on the call with the Horsemen is Richard Land. Land is a lobbyist who represents the sixteen million members of the Southern Baptist Convention and is a close friend of Bush's from Texas. Bush's loyalty to his friends is renowned, and in Land's case it sticks—every year Bush gives an address to the Baptist Convention's annual meeting, ensuring them he has their back on the inside. On Tuesday, June 21, 2005, President Bush addressed the Southern Baptist Convention for the fourth year in a row. In his statement via satellite, Bush called for a constitutional ban on same-sex marriage and reaffirmed his opposition to abortion.

Land isn't the only one representing born-again Christians on the Horsemen conference call. From the National Association of Evangelicals, Ted Haggard rings in, too. He represents forty-three thousand churches and thirty million members nationally. Haggard is the author of numerous popular Christian books—including *Primary Purpose: Marking it Hard for People to Go to Hell from Your City*. He says of his fellow evangelicals, "We have direct access...I can call [Tim Goeglein, Bush's deputy director of the Office of Public Liason], he'll take my concern to the president and get back to me in twenty-four hours!"

It doesn't matter that Bush isn't on the line. "Bush doesn't just understand our issues; he shares our worldview," Land explains. "What people are overlooking," one White House staffer concurs, "is that [Bush's] values are the same as the evangelicals'. He considers himself one of them. He doesn't need anyone to push him in their direction. He's already there. "

BUSH'S BELIEFS

President Bush is a self-described born-again Christian. His spiritual transformation, he says, took place when he turned forty, renounced alcohol, and found God. His spirituality doesn't only affect his personal life, though. After a sermon by Pastor Mark Craig of the First United Methodist Church in Austin in 1999, which Bush claims forever changed his life, the then governor of Texas told several evangelicals, "I believe that God wants me to be president." When Richard Land says Bush shares his worldview, he's not exaggerating.

Members of the religious Right aren't afraid to voice their opinions in the political realm. Tony Perkins, of the Family Research Council, has a lot of listeners for his skewed worldview, which includes bigoted arguments based on quack science. In 2004 the Family Research Council published a book called *Getting It Straight: What the Research Shows About Homosexuality*. The book challenges the notion that homosexuality is natural or genetic and tries to further the idea that sexual orientation is directly related to childhood abuse. Furthermore, the book cites studies and statistics that show homosexuality can lead to cancer and other illnesses. Sounds like he's been taking medical school courses taught by Dr. Bill Frist.

The religious Right is bigger, more powerful, and better organized than ever before. With its help a fellow born-again was put into the White House. Twice. Prior to the 2004 election, Karl Rove committed himself to the task of drawing 4 million more evangelical voters to the polls than he did in 2000, and that's exactly what happened. Bush won by a little less than 3.5 million popular votes, 4 million votes more than his popular vote difference in 2000 (when he received 500,000 less than Gore). Grassroots canvassing by local religious organizations was the major reason for this gain. Rove's efforts, though effective, were overshadowed by the work of thousands of community churches.

Under federal law, churches are forbidden from endorsing specific candidates. So Dr. D. James Kennedy can't stand in front of his ten-thousand-member congregation and shout, "Vote for Bush!" But he *can* steer people in a particular direction. He can talk about the importance of a "culture of life," of restoring

America to its "Christian roots." It doesn't take a genius to know which presidential candidate he's talking about.

Some churches are more direct. Chan Chandler, pastor of the East Waynesville Baptist Church in North Carolina, told his congregants to support his political views or leave his church, causing forty congregants to depart in protest in May of 2005. "If anyone there was planning on voting for John Kerry, they should leave," explained one former member, paraphrasing Chandler.

The Christian Coalition, founded in 1988 by Pat Robertson, simply went to the presses with "voter guides." The coalition disguises these guides as bipartisan. The lie works. The 1994 Republican revolution, in which Republicans took over both houses of Congress for the first time in forty years, was attributed to these very guides. Masterminded by Ralph Reed, the president of the Coalition at that time, forty-five million voter guides were sent to voters in 1996; in 2000, seventy-five million were sent. The 2004 guide, which was sent to thirty million households, made it very clear who God wanted Americans to vote for. Kerry had "no response" to "unrestricted abortion on demand." Bush, naturally, opposed it. Kerry supported "affirmative action that provides preferential treatment." Bush opposed it. You get the idea. The coalition also has a ratings system for current politicians, from 0 to 100 depending on a pol's allegiance to Christian Coalition values. The ratings are based on whether a politician voted for or against ten particular "pro-family" bills. Unsurprisingly, all the 0 ratings went to Democrats and the 100s to Republicans.

Ten years after the success of their voting guides, the coalition was at it again. The religious Right clearly got what it wanted

How this happened is a testament to the radical Right's
tight—and careful—control. Jay Sekulow, one of the Horsemen,
told thousands of pastors to make the election a central focus
of their sermons. Although he told them they "should avoid"
endorsing a candidate by name, everything else was fair game.
"We told them they were absolutely free and should encourage
people to vote their convictions," Sekulow explains .

Under current federal law, churches are forbidden from
endorsing specific candidates. Rev. Jerry Falwell has skirted this
line on several occasions, and his *Old Time Gospel Hour* lost its
tax exemption for 1986 and 1987 after the IRS determined that
the ministry was used for partisan politics. Despite this, Falwell
continues to use his position for political purposes. In 2004,
he sent out a "Falwell Confidential" e-mail soliciting support
from "conservative people of faith" for the Bush-Cheney ticket.
Another complaint has been filed, but its status is unknown at the
present. It will be interesting to see how vigilant enforcement of
the rules on tax-exempt religious organizations campaigning for
specific tickets will be in the current atmosphere in Washington.

There is a strong movement afoot in the House of
Representatives that would pull down this barrier between church
and politics. Representative Walter Jones, a Republican from
North Carolina, introduced HR 235, the House of Worship Free
Speech Restoration Act, in January of 2003. The act, if passed
into law, would allow churches to disseminate overtly political
messages from the pulpit. Under the provisions of this proposed
law, Jay Sekulow's nearly fifty thousand churches could openly
endorse candidates.

Another bill that would combine church and state is the Constitution Restoration Act, introduced by Senator Richard C. Shelby of Alabama. The act would make it illegal for any federal court to interfere in a matter related to "God as the sovereign source of law, liberty, or government." This vague wording would prevent judges from ruling in any religious or moral matter. Furthermore, any judge who goes against the act would be impeached. Tony Perkins and James Dobson, the cronies in the secret meeting at the Willard, would be ecstatic.

These laws are the ultimate goals of the religious Right, *and they are currently being debated in Congress.* If enacted, they will essentially eliminate the separation of church and state and mark a clear step forward in the ultraconservative pursuit of a theocracy.

That's precisely what the religious Right wants. To them, there is no such thing as a separation between religious and political America. When Tony Perkins struts across his stage and laments the state of America, when Pat Robertson shakes his fist into the camera on *The 700 Club*, they are not just trying to eliminate church-state separation but also claiming its existence was myth in the first place. Church and state, to these men, should be one—*this* is their vision for America. The founding fathers, they insist, were zealous Christians intent on founding a Christian nation—never mind the enormous body of historical evidence to the contrary

If the facts contradict their beliefs, they rewrite American history. If evolution doesn't support the creation myth, they nix it from textbooks. If judges don't act in their interests, they're God-in the reactionary Right's quest to make America in its image.

PLEASE DON'T SMITE TINKY WINKY...

It isn't unusual for Pat Robertson, founder of the Christian Coalition and the American Center for Law and Justice, to make incendiary remarks, but this time he went too far. On Tuesday, August 2, 2005, on his television program *The 700 Club*, Robertson tried to enlist God in the reactionary Right's quest for the federal judiciary. "Father," he began, "Lord, the government is in your hand, the rulers are in your hand... we pray, Lord, that this one key area of our government might be dramatically changed, that we might see people who respect the Constitution and who respect the fundamental law of the land." He continued, reaching a crescendo, "Take control, Lord! We ask for additional vacancies on the court!"

Was Robertson praying for God to smite our federal judges?

Jerry Falwell is another televangelist with a political aim. Falwell once "outed" Tinky Winky, a children's television character, because of his purple color and triangular antennae, and doesn't hesitate to make outrageous claims. This one is in regards to a much more serious subject, the terrorist attacks on September 11, 2001:

The abortionists have got to bear some burden for this, because God will not be mocked. And when we destroy forty million little innocent babies, we make God mad.

I really believe that the pagans, and the abortionists, and the feminists, and the gays and the lesbians who are actively trying to make that an alternative lifestyle, the ACLU, People for the American Way, all of them who have tried to secularize America, I point the finger in their face and say: you helped this happen.

When Falwell made the above statement on *The 700 Club*, Robertson agreed unequivocally, stating, "I totally concur."

THE FUNDAMENTALS

The father of American evangelism was an Anglican preacher named George Whitefield, who traveled throughout the colonies . His open suspicion of wealth and worldliness appealed to rural pioneer immigrants, and his persuasive sermons about the gospel in action united different Protestant factions throughout the colonies.

Over a century later, Lyman and Milton Stewart, oil tycoon brothers from California, put together and published *The Fundamentals*—a series of religious pamphlets that advertised a highly conservative religious doctrine. The Stewart brothers believed science and psychology clouded Whitefield's evangelism, and their pamphlets (and their title) become the foundation of Fundamentalism.

The five original Fundamentalist doctrines are:
1. Scripture's infallibility
2. The deity of Christ
3. Christ's virgin birth
4. The atonement achieved through Christ's death
5. Christ's literal resurrection and literal return in the second coming

In the twenties, H.L. Mencken remarked that if you were to throw an egg out of a train window anywhere in America, you would surely hit a Fundamentalist. But after the Scopes "monkey trial" in 1925, the movement, varied as it was, fell out of favor and

Fundamentalism has returned to prominence, particularly in the South. Catholics account for the majority of Fundamentalist converts. Hispanics are its fastest growing demographic.

Though Christ's second coming was expected before the millennium, once he does arrive, some evangelicals believe he will return to rule earth in peace for a thousand years. Others are convinced he will carry the souls of the devout up to heaven in the Rapture while the wicked are judged and the earth is destroyed.

	Current Leadership	Founded	Membership	Budget
Alliance Defense Fund (ADF)	President and General Counsel Alan Sears	In 1993 by Bill Bright, Larry Burkett, Rev. D. James Kennedy, Marlin Maddoux and James Dobson	Has trained over 700 lawyers; currently has 11 board members and 65 paid employees in 5 regional service centers	Approximately $16 million annually
American Center for Law & Justice (ACLJ)	Executive Director and Chief Counsel Jay Sekulow	In 1990 by Pat Robertson in Virginia Beach, VA	Over 500,000 members with 8 board members, 12 senior attorneys and 50 paid employees	$15.9 million in 2003
American Family Association (AFA)	Chairman Rev. Donald Wildmon and son, Vice President Tim Wildmon	In 1977 by Rev. Donald Wildmon	Claims 500,000 members; has 100 employees with state directors in 21 states	IRS returns in 2004 show $14.2 million in revenue
Campaign for Working Families PAC	President and Chairman Gary Bauer	In 1996 by Gary Bauer, former Family Research Council president and 2000 US presidential candidate	N/A	By 1998, was the country's 5th largest PAC, raising over $7 million in two years; spent $800,000 in the 2001-02 election cycle

Mission	Media Reach
The ADF sees itself as a divinely ordained legal group, working through the justice system to promote "traditional" family values. Its goals include dissolving gay families, forbidding them from forming in the first place, ending reproductive rights, and allowing Christians to proselytize in workplaces and on public property, including schools.	Daily newsletters, educational pamphlets, radio shows, online store and hourly email updates to members.
The arch-conservative response to the ACLU. It has an anti-abortion and anti-gay marriage/ partnership stance, and offers free services in the name of Christ. Christianity and patriotism are one and the same at the ACLJ, so it fights to end the separation of church and state--both on public property and in public funding. Encourages church leaders to tell their congregants who to vote for, and strongly advocates the Federal Marriage Amendment.	"Jay Sekulow Live!" airs weekdays on over 550 US radio stations. Sekulow has his own weekly show on the Trinity Broadcasting Network. He is also a regular guest on ABC, CBS, NBC, CNN, FOX, MSNBC, CNBC, and PBS. ACLJ also created the European Centre for Law and Justice and the Slavic Centre for Law and Justice.
The AFA aims to censor Television and Hollywood, and ban premarital sex, abortion, the National Endowment of the Arts, Disney, American Airlines, pornography and swearing.	AFA Journal with monthly circulation of 180,000, owns 200-station radio network across US. AFA Superstore sells everything from bumper stickers that say "Remember Terri" to videos called "It's Not Gay." Wildmon is a regular guests on morning, news, and talk shows.
Promotes ultraconservative candidates for office; so far has succeeded with Tom DeLay, Trent Lott, John Ashcroft, Dick Armey, Rick Santorum, and Roy Moore. In 2000, 83% of their slated candidates won.	N/A

	Current Leadership	Founded	Membership	Budget
Christian Coalition of America (CCA)	President Roberta Combs	In 1989 by Pat Robertson, also former president	They claim around 2 million members, but recent controversy has reduced it to roughly 500,000	Plagued by scandal, CAA's contributions fell from a high of $26.5 million in 1996 to about $3 million in 2000
Concerned Women for America	Founder and Chairwoman Beverly LaHaye	In 1979	Over 600,000 members	$11.6 million in revenue
Family Research Council	President Tony Perkins	In 1983 by Dr. James Dobson; later headed by Gary Bauer.	Receives approximately 20,000 membership requests per month	$10.2 million in revenue
Focus on the Family	President Dan Hodel	In 1977 by Dr. James Dobson	1.2 million member mmailing list and staff of 1,300	$136.6 million in revenue
Coral Ridge Ministries	Dr. D. James Kennedy	Church founded in 1960; Media Outreach founded in 1974	9,000 congregants; average audience of 3.5 million for broadcast televised services	The church took in $22.45 million in 2004; Ministries Media took in $37.76 million in 2003

Mission	Media Reach
The CCA wants to claim America for Christ, by pressuring Congress, training leaders, evangelizing, saturating the media with their messages, and convincing Christians that they're oppressed to galvanize voter turnout in their favor. The executive director of the New York CCA recently advised that homosexuality is worse for you than smoking.	Pat Robertson affiliates include 700 Club, Christian Broadcasting networks, ACLJ, and Regent University. Creates and distributes voter guides for every major federal and state election.
Through political advocacy aims to end abortion, pass a Constitutional amendment banning same-sex marriage, promote absintence-only education, forbid the teaching of evolution, and withdraw the US from the UN.	Daily radio show, "Concerned Women Today" on 75 stations with audience over 1 million.
Lobbying group with particular interest in the federal courts to promote an end to abortion, gay marriage, etc. Recently spearheaded "Justice Sunday" and "Justice Sunday II" to convince Congress to approve Bush's stalled judiciary nominees.	"Washington Watch," published monthly and "Family Policy," published bi-monthly. FRC affiliates include the Center for Human Life and Bioethics and the Center for Marriage and Family. FRC Action is the legislative lobbying offshoot.
A multi-media empire with its own university, literature, and version of history. Helps evanglicals get involved in the political process and also heal their homosexuality. Aims to co-opt public schools and institute prayer and tax credits. Leads censorship campaigns against multiculturalism, PTAs, homosexuality in the classroom and sex-ed. Also opposes hate-crime legislation.	2.3 million subscribers to 10 monthly magazines. Dobson on more than 3000 radio facilities in North America, in 15 languages, on about 6,300 facilities in 116 countries— reaching more than 200 million people daily. Dobson has written more than 17 books.
A television, print, and radio outreach program to help its audience learn how to take back every aspect of society for Christ, including schools, government, media, the workplace, history, and the legal system (to function under biblical law). Holds that every part of life must be reclaimed for Jesus or Armegeddon is near.	"Coral Ridge Hour" airs on more than 400 stations, 4 cable networks, and to 165 nations on the Armed Forces Network. More than 744 radio facilities nationwide broadcast 'Truths That Transform'. Altogether, some 3.5 million people listen weekly to CRM programming on radio or television.

	Current Leadership	Founded	Membership	Budget
Center for Christian Statesmanship	Founder and President Dr. D. James Kennedy	In 1995	Distinguished Christian Statesman Award given every year. Recipients: John Ashcroft, Judge Roy Moore, Majority Leader Dick Armey, Rep. Tom DeLay, etc.	Undisclosed
National Association of Evangelicals	Chairman Bill Hamel and President Ted Haggard	In 1942	Represents 51 member denomina- tions and 250 different evangeli- cal organizations; includes 45,000 local churches and 3 million people	$42.7 million in revenue in 2004
Chalcedon Foundation	President Mark R. Rushdoony	In 1965 by Rev. R.J. Rushdoony (1916- 2001)		
Southern Baptist Convention/public policy arm For Faith & Family	SBC chairman Rob Zinn. Dr. Richard Land - president of the Ethics and Religious Liberty Commission	Organized in 1845 in Augusta, GA	16 million members in more than 42,000 churches in the US. Also active internationally	$1.05 million in income in 2004

Mission	Media Reach
Center to promote Christian virtue and dogma on Capitol Hill through Christian outreach to politicians and staff.	Monthly "Washington Prayer Bulletin", online bookstore.
Represent the evangelical community to extend the kingdom of God and biblical truth.	Official affiliates include the Young Evangelicals Leadership Institute, World Relief, Christian Association of Prime Timers, Gospel Communications Network, International Day of Prayer for the Persecuted Church, and Internetevangelismday.com. The NAE published a Bible that sold 50 million English-language copies in 10 yrs.
A Christian reconstruction organization aimed at redefining literally every aspect of public life to Christian ends, with the goal of making evangelical Christianity the rule of law. Advocates the death penalty for homosexuals.	"Chalcedon Report" monthly magazine. Video and audio cassettes (nearly 1,000 tapes available now), books, journals, symposia, monographs, and pamphlets.
Similar goals to above organizations—aims to promote Christian doctrine in government and eliminate separation of church and state.	"For Faith & Family's Insight" and "For Faith and Family" radio broadcasts weekly to 1.5 million listeners on 600 radio stations. "Richard Land Live!" is a 3-hr live weekend program. Land's latest book is, *Imagine! A God-Blessed America* and in 2004, *Real Homeland Security*. "Baptist Press" is the SBC's daily newswire with 1.16 millino subscribers.

HONEST ABE

On a cold February day in 1864, a group of delegates from the National Reform Association buttoned their coats, put on their hats, and said a prayer before they headed to a meeting with President Abraham Lincoln. The ink was barely dry on their proposal for a constitutional amendment, but the delegates were fairly confident of its success. John Alexander, the leader of the new lobbying group, looked over the text and hoped that this new preamble would correct the founders' error at long last:

We, the people of the United States, humbly acknowledging Almighty God as the source of all authority and power in civil government, the Lord Jesus Christ as the Governor among the Nations, and His revealed will as of supreme authority, in order to constitute a Christian government...do ordain and establish this Constitution for the United States of America.

The scene was reminiscent of the ratification battles seventy-five years earlier. In the mid-nineteenth century, Protestant clergymen like Alexander increasingly claimed that the Constitution's indifference to Christianity would cause the nation's demise. The outbreak of the Civil War seemed to substantiate that, fanning fear that God was punishing America until the country recognized his divine law as supreme.

President Lincoln often quoted the Bible, and he had even

ordered the military to observe the Sabbath as a day of rest.
But what Alexander and these delegates did not know was that
President Lincoln was a Deist, just like the founding fathers. Nor
was he a particular fan of Christianity. As one of his business
partners had said, the president "went further against Christian
beliefs and doctrines and principles than any man I ever heard;
he shocked me. " Although Lincoln knew the scriptures well, he
never belonged to a church, privately disdained Christian clergy,
and believed avidly in evolution.

As Lincoln listened to the delegates that day, he probably
thought back thirty years to when he had written a book on
infidelity that doubted "the divinity of Christ." In the last
fourteen months of his life, Lincoln never so much as mentioned
their proposal.

CHAPTER TWELVE
THE BAPTISM OF OUR FOUNDERS

In the eye of the rotunda of the United States Capitol, a canopy fresco depicts the father of our country in the company of angels. He looks down from heaven, or in this case, down 180 feet onto tour guide David Barton. The crowd has gathered for a "fresh perspective on our nation's religious heritage," and Barton delivers with a story from George Washington's days on earth.

When he resigned his post as commander in chief of the Continental Army, Washington wrote a farewell letter to the governors of the thirteen states. He closed it with an "earnest prayer," asking God to keep the states in his holy protection. He reminded the governors that without humbly imitating "the Divine Author of our blessed Religion...we can never hope to be a happy Nation."

Barton translates in a folksy manner. "If we don't imitate Christ we won't be a happy nation. That is Washington!" He directs the tour's attention to the murals that circle the rotunda. "You've got two prayer meetings, a Bible study, and a baptism." He points toward Chapman's *The Baptism of Pocahontas* and shuttles the tour in front of Trumbull's *Declaration of Independence*.

"Isn't it interesting," Barton asks, "that we have all been trained to recognize the two least religious founding fathers?"

He motions to likenesses of Benjamin Franklin and Thomas Jefferson as they stand before John Hancock. "Compared to today's secularists, these two guys look like a couple of Bible-thumping evangelicals!" To underscore this point, Barton reveals how Jefferson signed letters "in the year of Our Lord Christ."

"What would happen if George Bush did that?" asks Barton. "They'd rip his head off!" A passerby interrupts Barton's tour and introduces himself as a member of the House of Representatives. "You don't get tour guides like this around here very often," he says, "and I had to stop and listen. You all are lucky to get to hear him."

Actually, Barton's unofficial Capitol tour is wildly popular among congressmen. According to Barton, they are "shocked" by the revelations of his "spiritual tour. " "I'm going to say 90 percent of those guys are absolutely floored at what they see," reveals Barton, "and out of the 90 percent, half of them are angry. It's always been, 'Why haven't I been taught this? Why didn't I know this?'"

Majority leader Bill Frist was so moved he called Barton "an inspiration" and invited every member of the Senate to join him on a tour. "He's rediscovering the spiritual roots of this nation," said Senator Sam Brownback. "His research provides the philosophical underpinning for a lot of the Republican effort in the country today—bringing God back into the public square. "

Having grown up, in his words, a "ranch kid," Barton is awed by his opportunity to teach Washington's powerbrokers. "Why in the heck would I know the president of the United States? Why should I know the majority leader of the House and Senate? Why do I know governors all over the nation?"

The answer is simple: because David Barton is the champion of a revisionist history aimed at destroying the ideological foundations of America and rebuilding them in the image of the Republican Right.

Among the wildflowers on an Aledo, Texas, prairie stands WallBuilders, a two-story building that serves as Barton's headquarters. The multimillion-dollar organization aims to develop public policies that "reflect biblical values" and educate the nation "concerning the godly foundation of our country." With the blessing of political cohorts, Barton is poised to do just that.

The chairwoman of the Texas Republican Party says her organization works "hand-in-glove " with WallBuilders. It's a snug fit since Barton serves as the state party's vice chairman. His efforts were crucial to its gains in the 2004 elections. He helped Governor Rick Perry enlist 1,000 "Patriot Pastors" on a crusade to register 300,000 "Value Voters."

Barton maintains close ties with key conservative leaders on the national level and advised House majority leader Tom DeLay on the Pledge Patriot Act, a piece of legislation that summarizes Barton's agenda. During the McCarthy era, congressmen were so eager to show the public that they were God-fearing warriors against Communism, they voted to change the Pledge of Allegiance into a prayer by adding two words.

The Pledge Patriot Act was designed to keep "One nation, *under God"* in the pledge. Barton's goal is to make this phrase the foundation of American government. He claims that the separation between church and state came not from our founding fathers but from the 1963 Supreme Court ruling against prayer in public schools.

To combat the Court's "judicial activism" and return the country to what he believes was the original intent of our founders, Barton seeks ammunition on the shelves of the WallBuilders library. Applying an anecdotal approach to history, Barton searches through thousands of books and scans through years of colonial newspapers. He cobbles together what he believes was the "true" intent of the framers of the Constitution.

"The founders said we are a Christian nation," claims Barton. "Those are their words." A master of the selective quote, Barton uses statements by the founding fathers to baptize them, one by one, as born-agains.

Barton cites that Thomas Jefferson called himself, "a real Christian, that is to say, a disciple of the doctrines of Jesus." Being a disciple of the *doctrines* of Jesus is one matter, but Jefferson's definition of a "real Christian" certainly doesn't fit Barton's.

"To the corruptions of Christianity I am, indeed, opposed," Jefferson wrote. Evoking Jesus for partisan politics would certainly fit into this category, but his views on the subject went deeper. To discover the true teachings of Jesus, Jefferson told John Adams, one had to abstract his words "from the rubbish in which it is buried," which was "as separable from that as the diamond from the dunghill."

Believing that kings and priests transformed the ethical teachings of Jesus into "abracadabra," Jefferson took a razor to his own Bible by candlelight. He removed the letters of Paul, Jude, John, and Peter and extracted all of the miracles of Jesus. He was left with a book that had no miracles: no resurrection, no annunciation, and no virgin birth.

Crying blasphemy would fail to serve Barton's purpose. Instead, he claims Jefferson's hatchet job was simply to publish the "red letter" portions of the New Testament "in order to introduce the Indians to Christian morality." Barton's gross oversimplification incorrectly paints Jefferson as a fellow evangelical. This is untrue, though Jefferson did have religious beliefs.

In the words of one historian, Jefferson was "mesmerized" by religion. It "enraged him, tantalized him, alarmed him, and sometimes inspired him." But Jefferson only accepted a belief if it could pass the test of Enlightenment philosopher John Locke. If the belief could not bear the scrutiny of rationality, it could not be accepted as truth.

Jefferson believed in a God of reason. Only when unreasonable notions were taken out of the New Testament could Jefferson become, as Barton points out, a disciple of the doctrines of Jesus. Jefferson would praise these moral and ethical teachings as "the most pure, benevolent, and sublime which have ever been preached to man."

Barton is right in that Jefferson signed his letters "in the year of Our Lord Christ." What he fails to mention is that this was a standard signature of the time. He also neglects to translate the phrase into Latin. *Anno Domini Nostri Iesu Christi* is, in short, *AD*.

The liberties taken with our founders continue with Thomas Paine, author of *Common Sense*. Barton claims Paine "forcefully asserts that it is 'the error of schools' to teach sciences without 'reference to the Being who is author of them.'" By disguising the man behind the quote, Barton is able to craft Thomas Paine as a kindred spirit on creationism in the classroom.

The truth is that Thomas Paine believed Christianity "a fable, which, for absurdity and extravagance is not exceeded by any thing that is to be found in the mythology of the ancients." If this is true, how could Paine advocate the inclusion of God in science classes?

Thrown into a Parisian prison during France's Age of Terror, Paine began writing *The Age of Reason*, a scathing romp against Christianity and a celebration of the rational mind. The book is a culmination of Paine's belief in the teachings of John Locke, Francis Bacon, and physicist Isaac Newton. Like Locke on belief and Bacon on knowledge, Newton applied the test of rationality to science.

Newton believed that the universe was governed by a set of unbending laws that could be deduced by reason. By searching for these laws, Newton discovered that the same force bringing apples to the ground kept planets orbiting around the sun. He found clockwork precision in the "chaos" of the cosmos.

Men of the Enlightenment thrilled at Newton's union of heaven and earth. If the universe operated like a clock, reason could uncover the designs of the watchmaker. Communion with the divine could be achieved, not through priests and mystics, but through equations and rational thinking. Science was charged with the divine, and Paine believed it was necessary to integrate God's rational intent when teaching the operations of his machine.

"Are we to have no word of God—no revelation?" wrote Paine in *The Age of Reason*. "I answer, yes; there is a word of God; there is a revelation. The word of God is the creation we behold, and it is in this word, which no human invention can counterfeit or alter, that God speaketh universally to man."

To Paine, the study of the universe *was* the study of a divine creation. The two were intertwined. Only Paine was careful not to evoke the Christian deities of Jesus or the Holy Ghost when discussing God. Like many of our founding fathers, he referred to a "Creator of the Universe" or "Divine Artist" or a "Supreme Architect." This was because Paine was not a Christian. He was a Deist.

"The religion of Deism is superior to the Christian Religion," reasoned Paine. A product of the Enlightenment, Deism relied on reason by taking the worldview of Newton's mechanical universe. According to Paine, Deism was "free from all those invented and torturing articles that shock our reason." He went on to say that its creed is pure and "sublimely" simple. "It believes in God, and there it rests."

Though Paine was more radical in his belief than other founders, Deism greatly influenced the thinking and works of the best of them. The Declaration of Independence, written by Jefferson and signed by John Adams and Benjamin Franklin, refers not to Christ but to "Nature's God" and the "Creator."

A wonderful explanation of this belief system appeared in *The Week* magazine on June 10, 2005 entitled The Faith of the Framers:

"Less a religion than a way of perceiving divinity in the world, Deism is rooted in the 17th and 18th century scientific and philosophical revolutions of the Enlightenment. For deists, God is not a father figure that dwells in Heaven and performs miracles. Rather, he is an undefined and unknowable 'prime mover' who

reveals himself in immutable laws that can rationally explain both cosmic and human affairs. Everything from the physical forces that govern the universe to the essential freedom of man, deists believe, are outward signs of God's presence among us. In keeping with their deist beliefs, the Founders often refrained from calling the source of their inspiration 'God'. He—or rather it—was, "Divine Providence" and "The Universal Sovereign" among other euphemisms."

This explains the use of "The Creator" in our constitution as well as many similar references in public prayers, letters and other writings by these men.

Jefferson and Adams discovered Deism during their college years. At William and Mary, the center of Deist thought in Virginia, Jefferson was taught Locke, Newton, and Bacon by a clergyman who hailed from the Enlightenment tradition in Scotland. At Harvard, John Adams gave up his ambitions to become a minister after an Enlightenment-influenced pastor awakened him to the dogma of organized religion.

While Jefferson and Adams grew up with more liberal strains of Christianity, Benjamin Franklin was raised in the strict tradition of New England Calvinism. Though Franklin never attended college, he began reading Deist authors at an early age. At thirteen, he wrote his parents, "I think vital religion has always suffered when orthodoxy is more regarded than virtues." His father was even more distressed when Benjamin turned to Deism at fifteen.

In his last years, Franklin shied from the hard-line Deism of his youth, but when asked about his religious beliefs five weeks before his death, Franklin replied, "I believe in one God, Creator of the Universe: That he governs the World by his Providence. That he ought to be worshipped. That the most acceptable Service we can render to him is doing good to his other Children." With the exception of man being governed by providence, Jefferson and Adams shared Franklin's view of God.

Jefferson, like Franklin, eventually reconciled Deism with the Christian faith. Later in life, Jefferson mellowed enough to consider the possibility of life after death. He attended services of a liberal Unitarian church in Philadelphia. By practicing a faith that valued reason over dogma, Jefferson rejoiced at how "this blessed country of free inquiry in belief" had seen the revival of "the genuine doctrine of only one God." Ever optimistic in man's reason, Jefferson trusted that "there is not a young man now living who will not die a Unitarian."

Jefferson found a home in the Unitarian church because the church embraced, in essence, Christian Deism. David Barton would deem this an oxymoron. "What is a Deist?" Barton asks. "In dictionaries like Webster's," he reveals, "agnostic" and "atheist" appear as synonyms of Deism. By viewing the founders between these narrow poles, Barton denies *any* were Deists.

Barton's argument is as wrong as defining the word "evangelical" by two of its synonyms, "dogmatic" and "bigoted." Just as evangelical Catholics and evangelical Protestants exist today, Deist Christians existed in colonial times. These men had faith in an omnipresent God, but felt religious dogma divided believers more than it unified them.

John Adams, also a Unitarian, was "a church-going animal " and attended services twice on Sundays. Like Jefferson, Adams was a disciple of the doctrines of Jesus. He even believed that Franklin's protégé Thomas Paine had gone too far with his antagonistic views toward Christianity. Dogma, however, frustrated Adams to the point where he wrote Jefferson, "This would be the best of all possible Worlds, if there were no Religion in it."

Like the other founding fathers, Adams viewed religion as a necessary tool for personal growth, which is why he continued his quote by writing, "without Religion this World would be Something not fit to be mentioned in polite Company, I mean Hell." Adams also knew that religion belonged in its own arena.

Even though Deism relied on individual reason over sacred texts, neither Adams nor the other prominent founding fathers wanted to press it upon Americans any more than they did Christianity, Buddhism, or Hinduism. Jefferson was so insistent on this point that he abolished the divinity school at his alma mater, in spite of its heavy Deist influence.

Jefferson replaced the divinity professors with those who taught science and law, and when he encountered resistance to further changes at William and Mary, he packed up and created his own university. Jefferson made sure that the University of Virginia had no chaplain and no religious curriculum. By choosing James Madison to join him on the university's board, Jefferson knew his edict would be supported.

Episcopalian bishop William Meade was a close friend of Madison and other Virginian founding fathers and wrote that it was his impression that Madison's "creed was not strictly regulated

by the Bible." Meade also writes, "Whatever may have been the
private sentiments of Mr. Madison on the subject of religion, he
was never known to declare any hostility to it. He always treated
it with respect." For Madison, this point was more important than
any declaration of his personal faith.

James Madison was raised in a devout Anglican family in
Virginia. Rather than have their son attend school with the Deists
at William and Mary, his parents sent him away to study with the
orthodox Christians at the College of New Jersey. When Madison
returned home to Montpelier, he was horrified to witness that his
own church was throwing religious dissenters into jail.

This moment convinced Madison that religious freedom
was essential to a democratic state. While drafting Virginia's
constitution in 1776, Madison fought to insure that it granted
freedom of conscience. Serving in the Virginia House of
Delegates, Madison helped defeat a bill that gave money to
religious organizations—a prelude to the battle he would wage a
decade later at the Constitutional Convention.

Madison clearly won that battle, but for some reason, David
Barton thinks he can go back and fight it. The Constitutional
Convention is the culmination of Barton's efforts to paint the
founding fathers as born-again Christians. He denies Madison
ever wanted the separation of church and state. He states that while
Madison alluded to a "wall of separation," that wall was simply to
keep Congress from enacting a national religion. He takes special
note of the fact that the words "church-state separation" do not
appear in the Constitution.

Barton also states that fifty-two of the fifty-five signers of the

Constitution were "orthodox, evangelical Christians" although he cites no evidence to support this. On the contrary, Clinton Rossiter wrote in *1787: The Grand Convention* that "although it had its share of strenuous Christians," the gathering "was largely made up of men in whom the old fires were under control or had even flickered out." By no means was the Constitutional Convention a revival meeting.

Barton takes careful note of Benjamin Franklin's request that the Convention open up with a prayer every morning. He fails to say that this issue wasn't even taken to a vote after one founder felt it would make them seem desperate in the public eye.

Perhaps the most ludicrous claim of Barton's is that our three branches of government originated from the Bible. He says founders drew the idea from Isaiah 33:22, which reads, "For the Lord is our judge, the Lord is our ruler, the Lord is our king; he will save us." Sorry, Barton, but none of the founders reference this or any other Bible verse. Locke and other Enlightenment thinkers are the real geniuses behind the separation of powers.

As many of the founders became presidents in the course of their public lives, Barton offers evidence to "prove" they ruled over a Christian nation. Barton states that President Washington was "an open promoter of Christianity," citing his letter of resignation as commander in chief. A careful reading of the letter reveals that Washington's words took the tone of Thomas Jefferson, not Jerry Falwell.

Washington wrote that it was his "earnest prayer" that God would "incline the hearts of the Citizens" to demean themselves "with that Charity, humility and patience, which were the Characteristicks of the Divine Author of our blessed Religion, and without an humble imitation of whose example in these things, we can never hope to be a happy Nation."

Washington is not saying that Americans must worship Christ. He is saying that without humbly imitating Christ's examples of charity, humility, and pacific temper of mind, citizens can never hope to live in a happy nation. Like Jefferson, he carefully limits his language on Jesus with the exactitude of legal jargon.

As for our second president, John Adams, Barton plasters Adams's declaration for a "Solemn Humiliation, Fasting and Prayer" on his web site. The proclamation reads that the "prosperity of nations ultimately and essentially depend on the protection and blessing of Almighty God." Aside from the fact that Adams is using the language of Deism, Barton fails to mention that a day of religious fasting was a colonial tradition.

The examples continue, but Barton confuses the issue by equating the personal beliefs of presidents with constitutional law. Presidents, just as any citizens, are allowed to express their personal faith in public. This is a right guaranteed by the First Amendment. But even in their public declarations, the founders were extraordinarily careful never to evoke the divine in the arena of public policy. The same does not hold true for Barton and the born-agains.

By scrounging for any mention, word, or hint of the divine in the annals of our founders, Barton builds an impressive historical spin job. Too bad the founders aren't available to spin back. For Barton to employ his colonial sideshow for the benefit of the extreme Right is odious enough, but the fact that Barton tries to incorporate his views in public schools is abhorrent.

Through his political connections, Barton has served as a consultant to the school boards of Texas and California. With his recent praises from the most powerful men in Congress, we can certainly expect the addition of a few more state boards.

On his Capitol tour, it's a shame that Barton doesn't focus on the true meaning behind another portrait in the rotunda. In the *Embarkation of the Pilgrims,* William Bradford, Miles Standish, and other pilgrims are depicted in the midst of prayer around an open Bible. They risk a treacherous voyage to the New World to escape the religious intolerance of England. Rather than reduce the scene to "a Bible study," Barton should focus on the tradition of religious freedom the pilgrims sought to achieve.

Ultimately, we can take comfort in the fact that our most prominent fathers were so influenced by Deism. The Constitutional Convention was a unique moment in history. It brought together a collection of minds that were more attuned to reason than ever before or perhaps ever after.

With a religious belief in the powers of the rational mind, the founders created the most reasoned and effective Constitution known to man. In essence, the Constitution provided the pinnacle document of their faith, a faith that insisted the laws of sacred texts never interfere with the laws of man.

To rewrite it in the image of David Barton and the religious Right *would* be heresy.

THE PLEDGE OF ALLEGIANCE: A MARXIST MANIFESTO?

The founding fathers didn't draft the Pledge of Allegiance. Neither did any president. In fact, most Americans, if asked who wrote the pledge, probably wouldn't know the answer.

And they would be surprised to find out it was written in 1892, by a Marxist Socialist named Francis Bellamy.

Not only is the origin of the pledge unusual—so was the original statement. Bellamy's pledge, written for the popular family-oriented magazine *Youth Companion*, didn't contain any reference to God. It didn't even mention America!

It wasn't until 1924 that the National Flag Conference added "of the United States of America" to the pledge. The change was adopted despite Francis Bellamy's objection.

In 1954, the Senate and House passed a bill, which Eisenhower signed, adding "under God" to the pledge. The bill was passed to "acknowledge the dependence of our people and our Government upon... the Creator... [and] deny the atheistic and materialistic concept of communism."

Since then, various movements have tried, and failed, to amend the pledge again. The most recent, by anti-abortion advocates, seeks to add "born and unborn" to its close. Bellamy would likely object.

Note, it wasn't until 1957, during the Red Scare, that "In God We Trust" became the motto on our money. Our founders

146   thought E Pluribus Unum—"from many, one"—was the better phrase, and so do I.

CHAPTER THIRTEEN

ONE NATION, UNDER THE RIGHT

When the state police raided the Old Hickory BBQ shack, home of the spiciest ribs in quaint Gibson County, they didn't intend to disrupt the balance of power among the three branches of the federal government. They did intend to arrest restaurateur Darrel Russelburg and his trio of waitresses (clad in three thongs and six latex nipple patches) in violation of Indiana's indecency law.

Russelburg argued that the state law was too vague, and claimed that an illegal display of buttocks could range anywhere from a "bikini" to a "plumber's crack." His broad interpretation did not sit well with the local jury. When the foreman read the verdict, Russelburg could almost hear the cries of victory in the community church. Its members had long rallied to shut down his business. Now they had done it with the power of the court.

Stepping outside the Gibson County Courthouse, the downcast Russelburg felt victim to local prejudice. When he looked up to the Ten Commandments monument in front of him, his spirits elevated with revenge. Russelburg called the Indiana Civil Liberties Union to file a complaint. Court cases, he said, "should be decided based on Indiana's laws and not on religious principles. "

"Founding fathers never intended to separate God from government," retorted Congressman John Hostettler at the "Keep the Commandments" rally on the east lawn of the courthouse. Though hundreds of people supported him, a federal district judge ruled otherwise. The U.S. Marshals were ordered to remove the monument by April 1, 2005.

In an appeal to the president, Hostettler asked Bush not to enforce the judge's order. It was unconstitutional, wrote Hostettler, and "inconsistent with both the clear intent of the Framers and the Christian heritage of the United States." When President Bush endorsed the judge's ruling, Hostettler turned to majority leader Tom DeLay.

Eager to set the record straight, DeLay said that House Republicans would use legislation to finally address the "incredibly confusing" doctrine on the separation of church and state. "To base decisions on religion upon a letter written by Thomas Jefferson and having no relevance to the Constitution," lamented DeLay, "gets you into this mess."

The "mess" DeLay refers to began with the earnest concerns of one of our nation's earliest religious minorities. In 1802, a group of Danbury Baptists wanted to ensure the new Constitution made no man suffer "in name, person, or effects on account of his religious opinions." President Jefferson calmed the fears of this Connecticut religious sect by writing that "religion is a matter which lies solely between man & his god."

Jefferson was an unwavering proponent of religious freedom. When drafting the Virginia Act for Establishing Religious Freedom, Jefferson wrote that "our civil rights have no dependence on our religious opinions, more than our opinions in physics or geometry."

In his letter to the Danbury Baptists, Jefferson continued with words that have been hotly debated over the years. The First Amendment, wrote Jefferson, was "a wall of separation between church and state." DeLay believes that since this phrase originated in a letter and not in the Constitution, the entire doctrine is null and void. By subscribing to David Barton's fabricated history, DeLay hides the reasons *why* the document is so silent on matters of religion.

At the time of the Constitutional Convention, America was a land of enormous religious diversity. Granted, the vast majority of citizens came from Protestant backgrounds, but denominations ranged from the Quakers of Pennsylvania to the Baptists of Virginia to the Congregationalists of Massachusetts. In the face of this diversity, the framers believed neither fire-and-brimstone Calvinists nor liberal Presbyterians could ever dominate national politics.

James Madison was so earnest in this conviction that he opposed the passage of the First Amendment during Virginia's convention to ratify the Constitution. Madison was no dogmatic fundamentalist. He was the premier defender of religious freedom in America. He simply believed religion had no place whatsoever in the Constitution. None. Man's spiritual beliefs were his own business.

Madison, whose spiritual growth sharpened his reason, could hardly imagine America getting caught up in a battle over the Ten Commandments. Neither could the other founders. The notion would be completely *irrational* to them. After all, the law of the land was the Constitution, not the Old Testament. The founders knew what they were doing when they left the words "God" and "Christ" out of the Constitution. Other omissions they couldn't forsee.

In the roaring twenties, Seattle bootlegger Roy Olmstead built an empire on illegal hootch. He had a fleet of sea vessels to bring it in, an underground bunker to store it, fifty people to sell it, and bookkeepers and attorneys to make the whole operation seem legal. In a bad month his racket took in two hundred grand. In a year it took in two million. Roy got half of everything.

There was only one problem. The feds kept his phones on wiretap, and stenographers transcribed enough evidence to put him away for a long time. Though the jig seemed up for Roy, his lawyers claimed wiretapping violated his Fourth Amendment rights.

In 1928, *Olmstead v. United States* went before the Supreme Court, and the question in front of the judges was whether or not the feds had violated Roy's constitutional rights. What does the Constitution specifically say on wiretapping? As much as it says on telephones or telegraphs. Nothing. How then can *any* decision be made in regard to wiretapping?

The founders knew they could not anticipate every conceivable issue that might brush up against the Constitution. Nor could they predict how technology would evolve. This is why they inserted "messy" language like "unreasonable search and seizures" into the Fourth Amendment.

In his dissenting opinion on *Olmstead v. United States*, Justice Louis Brandeis wrote that "the makers of our Constitution undertook to secure conditions favorable to the pursuit of happiness" and that the founders recognized the right for man to "be let alone." To protect that right, Brandeis wrote, "every unjustifiable intrusion by the government upon the privacy of the individual, whatever the means employed, must be deemed a violation of the Fourth Amendment."

Welcome to the living Constitution. The founders were smart enough to leave vague phrases in the document to allow breathing room for the country to grow. Many such phrases are in the Bill of Rights, the first ten amendments that Justice Robert Jackson called "majestic generalities." Others, like "equal protection" and "due process of law," are in the Fourteenth Amendment.

These brief, broad phrases weren't because the founders got too lazy to write a couple of extra words. When the founders wanted to be specific, they indicated precisely what they meant. This was the case when choosing the number thirty-five as the minimum age for the president.

The founders did not shackle the Constitution with an overkill of specifics. Their brilliance can be seen through the eyes of Alabamans, whose state constitution specified every specific detail its framers could imagine. State leaders wanted to draft a document that would never need amending. While the average length of a state constitution is 26,000 words (compared to about 18,700 for the U.S. Constitution), the Alabama document has over 310,000 words. Lo and behold, in its short life, this charter has been the most amended state constitution in America, with over 740 such changes as of 2004.

Our founding founders created phrases open to interpretation, and they created a branch of government to do just that. Founders intended for the Supreme Court to be the final verdict on the interpretation of the Constitution. In shaping their opinions, justices look back to the words of the founders for direction. Just as Brandeis evoked founders to interpret the Fourth Amendment in 1928, Justice Hugo Black evoked Thomas Jefferson to interpret the First Amendment in 1947.

The First Amendment reads, "Congress shall make no law respecting *an establishment of religion*," and to give authority to his ruling on this "establishment clause," Black turned to Jefferson's letter to the Danbury Baptists. Though the religious Right would have you believe otherwise, Black was spot on when he quoted Jefferson's "wall of separation" phrase.

The religious Right screams that separation of church and state was a post-World War II invention. They tell their believers that America has strayed from its days of Eden. They lay this blame on liberal judges like Hugo Black, who imposed their godless wills on a Christian nation.

There is a reason why Thomas Jefferson and other founders have suddenly appeared in the sound bites of Tom DeLay. With history lessons from David Barton, the religious Right claims that our evangelical founders envisioned One Nation Under Christ. To return to the days of this mythic yesteryear, all America needs to do is eliminate the heathen activists of the Supreme Court. Only then can "the wall between church and state" be torn down.

The fact is that this "wall of separation" *was* the intent of the founders. As I have discussed, as much as the founders revered the moral and ethical teachings of Jesus, they did not want a biblically based government. Instead, they followed their political mentor John Locke, who said, "There is absolutely no such thing, under the Gospel, as a Christian Commonwealth." In the Treaty of Tripoli in 1797, the Senate could not have been clearer when it stated: "The government of the United States is not in any sense founded on the Christian religion."

As James Madison argued, the separation was best for both state *and* church. If the government took no endorsement on religion, citizens were free to explore their own faiths without any intrusion or official sanction by the state.

Ultimately, however, the founders realized that the establishment clause was a necessary addition to the Constitution. Money was one issue. Given the Revolutionary War rallying cries against unfair taxation, it was only natural that citizens wanted assurance that no taxes went to churches they didn't believe in. Americans also had too many bad memories of religious persecution in Europe. Like the Danbury Baptists, they didn't want to leave anything to chance.

Given that presidents are also men, the boundaries on this wall of separation often slipped. But when George Washington offered a prayer for the nation and John Adams proclaimed his day of national fasting, Thomas Jefferson took them to task for it. He made no such pronouncements in his own presidency and refused to even enact a day of thanksgiving. While James Madison did concede to Thanksgiving in 1815, he regretted it in his diaries twenty years later.

Congress also operated under the assumption that church and state were separated. In 1810 it created the National Postal

Service and declared that mail would be delivered seven days a week. No congressman raised his voice to object that post offices would be open on the Sabbath. When the issue did come up before the Senate in 1828, Kentucky senator Richard Johnson issued a grave warning.

If postmen were to be given a day of rest, Johnson argued, Congress would have to choose between Saturday and Sunday. The choice would force them to declare which day was indeed the Sabbath. Johnson predicted that if the government started to decide what were "the laws of God," religious oppression could run rampant. Even those who opposed Johnson argued that choosing Sunday as a day off would not "form the justly odious combination of church and state."

The prudence of our earliest Congresses is completely absent from those who run it today. When DeLay isolates the "wall of separation" to one letter by Thomas Jefferson, he undermines the intent of our founders and lays bare his ignorance. The scary part is that to tear down the wall between church and state, DeLay is also tearing apart the checks and balances among our three branches of government.

Though Tom DeLay doesn't like the fact that a federal court asked U.S. Marshals to remove the Ten Commandments monument outside the Gibson County Courthouse, nowhere in the Constitution does he have the authority to do anything about it. But rather than accept defeat graciously by respecting the structure of checks and balances, Delay wants to change the rules of the game completely.

In his crusade to "Keep the Commandments," Rep. Hostettler

decided to add an unusual amendment to a House spending bill. The bill prohibits the allocation of any government funds for the enforcement of *Russelburg v. Gibson County*. What began with three half-nude waitresses in a barbecue shack may have profound implications for the nation.

The Supreme Court does not have the power of the purse. Congress does. Without any money to pay for the removal of the Ten Commandments monument, the U.S. Marshals are powerless to do anything about it. Hostettler's amendment sets a very dangerous precedent for the country.

Rather than rely on the Supreme Court to interpret the Constitution, Hostettler's amendment shifts that power to Congress. Because majority leader Tom DeLay saw fit to rely on his own interpretation of what is and isn't constitutional, he successfully passed Hostettler's amendment through the House.

Minority whip Steny Hoyers said the passage was "unfortunate." "Legislation which is designed to undercut the enforcement of the law as found by the courts," remarked Hoyers, "undermines a nation of laws." If DeLay wanted to address this "mess" between church and state, he created a bigger one by mucking up the Constitution.

Even the wet-naps from the Old Hickory BBQ Shack can't clean up that mess.

CHAPTER FOURTEEN

DEATH TO THE LIVING CONSTITUTION

When Tom DeLay boasts that Congress can "unset the courts" because they have the "power of the purse," he threatens to revert the federal judicial system to the sorry condition it was in over two centuries ago. In the years following the ratification of the Constitution, the Supreme Court did not convene in the grand marble building of today. It was exiled to a chamber in the basement of the Capitol. That was if justices were even available to *meet*.

Instead of addressing the weighty judicial matters of our new nation, justices on the Supreme Court were shipped off to sit on far-flung lower courts. Riding circuit literally meant riding on horseback across the backwoods and poor roads of America. "I cannot resolve to spend six months of the year," wrote Justice Thomas Johnson in his resignation letter to President Washington, "on roads at taverns chiefly and often in situations where the most moderate desires are disappointed."

Those able to endure this wearing job were met with petty issues at their destination. The hearings they sat on, dealing with property and contract disputes, were the kind that belong in today's small-claims courts. For men who were supposed to be on the highest court in the land, the task was an insult.

Who was responsible for the shabby state of our nation's judicial power? Congress. The Constitution left the creation of the lower courts to Congress, and Congress was stalling on its duties. By passing the law that made justices ride circuit in the first place, Congress treated the Supreme Court like an unwanted stepchild.

The fiery Alexander Hamilton predicted this kind of situation years before in *The Federalist Papers*. He was concerned that the judiciary had "no influence over either the sword or the purse." The president had the sword and Congress had the purse. The Supreme Court suffered at the whims of both.

When his Federalist Party took a hit in the 1801 elections, losing both Congress and the presidency, Hamilton feared the incoming Republicans would make *every* branch of government as weak as the judiciary. In their few weeks left in power, the Federalists made a last stab for the nation's future strength.

By passing the Judiciary Act of 1801, the lame-duck Congress eliminated the practice of circuit riding and created sixteen new circuit judgeships. With the help of another lame duck, President John Adams, these positions were filled with Federalists. In the last night before Thomas Jefferson took office, Adams scribbled appointments for these "midnight judges" until the wee hours of his presidency.

"The Federalists have retired into the judiciary as a stronghold," his successor wrote in a fury, "and from that battery all the works of republicanism are to be beaten down and erased." Backed by a Republican Congress, Jefferson set his sights on impeaching all of Adams's midnight judges.

Taking the soapbox in New York City, Jefferson's sworn

enemy railed against this plan. Congressional politics may have created the judgeships, argued Hamilton, but now that the posts were filled, Congress could not "abolish the judges at pleasure." If this happened, he warned, "the Constitution is gone; it is a dead letter."

Tough luck, the Republicans argued back, and Congress repealed the Judiciary Act. When Hamilton threatened to take the matter to the Supreme Court, Congress canceled the Court's next two sessions, put the justices back on their horses, and sent them off to the nether regions of circuit courts.

One rider, however, would return with a vengeance. As a young man of hearty stock, John Marshall had survived the freezing winter in Valley Forge under General Washington. Though he certainly had the to strength to ride circuit, he knew that the Supreme Court deserved better respect.

When the justices finally reconvened, Marshall, a staunch law-and-order Federalist, elevated the Court to its rightful place in history. "He hit the Constitution much as the Lord hit the chaos," remarked one contemporary , "at a time when everything needed creating."

Nobody expected this would all result from a minor matter concerning a justice of the peace. For the first time in America's history, the Supreme Court struck down a law of Congress as unconstitutional, and that came as quite a surprise to Congress and the president. (Interestingly, it was a law that sought to *expand* the Supreme Court's jurisdiction beyond Constitutional limits.) Jefferson denounced the "twistifications" of Marshall's ruling in *Marbury vs. Madison*. He called the Supreme Court a "subtle corps of sappers and miners constantly working underground to undermine the foundations of our confederated fabric." He reserved his best words for Marshall himself, who he scorned as "the Federalist serpent in the democratic Eden of our administration."

Tough luck, argued Marshall, "an act of the legislature repugnant to the Constitution is void." With one stroke, Marshall lifted the Supreme Court to its proper stature as an equal branch of government. After *Marbury vs. Madison*, the Supreme Court used this power of judicial review to abolish any law that was unconstitutional. Both the executive and legislative branches had to abide by its decision.

Though Hamilton argued in *The Federalist Papers* that the Supreme Court had this power of judicial review, the possibility was theoretical until Marshall decided to actually apply it. We should be grateful for his bold act, because judicial review has seen America through the most misguided and politically motivated laws of its legislatures.

One such law came after a "huge monster," as a publication of the time called it, churned down the Hudson River "vomiting fire and smoke from its throat." The maiden voyage of the *Clermont*, Robert Fulton's first steamboat, may have frightened those watching from the banks, but the New York legislature was all too pleased at the windfall for their state. They granted Fulton the exclusive right to handle all steamboat traffic for thirty years.

When Thomas Gibbons built his own boat, hired Cornelius Vanderbilt to run it, and charged passengers a cheaper fare, the state court forced him to stop. After *Gibbons v. Ogden* reached the

Supreme Court, the power of judicial review brought down Fulton's state-sanctioned monopoly. Justice Oliver Wendell Holmes realized the economic future of America would be destroyed if the New York law wasn't. Other uses of judicial review were not so wise.

The decision in *Dred Scott v. Sandford,* in the words of Chief Justice Charles Evans Hughes, was the nastiest of the Court's "self-inflicted wounds." Dred Scott was the personal slave of Dr. John Emerson of Missouri and accompanied this army surgeon on his travels down to Louisiana and Florida and over to the slave-free states of Illinois and Wisconsin Territory.

When Emerson died, Scott and his abolitionist lawyer went before a St. Louis county court. Because Scott technically resided in free states, they argued, he had the legal right to freedom. John Sanford, the brother of Emerson's widow, claimed otherwise. Scott won his freedom, but Sanford won an appeal to the Missouri Supreme Court.

Dred Scott's last chance at emancipation lay with the highest court in the land. His timing was unfortunate. On March 4, 1857, two days before the ruling on *Dred Scott v. Stanford* (Sanford's name misspelled by the court clerk), President James Buchanan gave his inaugural address. Buchanan had the spine of a wet noodle, and rather than address the looming crisis over slavery, he passed the buck to the Supreme Court where it would, "it is understood, be speedily and finally settled."

Chief Justice Roger Taney, who replaced John Marshall after thirty-four years of service, had none of the wisdom of his predecessor. He was a crotchety eighty-one-year-old who had once had slaves of his own. In *Dred Scott v. Stanford,* Taney wrote that Negroes were "so inferior that they had no rights which a white man was bound to respect." He ruled Scott didn't even have the right to a trial because he was merely property. Since the Fifth Amendment protected property, Congress could not deprive anyone of it.

Dred Scott v. Stanford showed the dark side of judicial review, and the Republican Right points to the case as a clear reason why such review should be abolished. "With typical activist flair," writes Mark Levin in his screed *Men In Black: How the Supreme Court is Destroying America*, "Taney overruled Congress's power to ban slavery in the territories and imposed his own view on the nation."

The Supreme Court, like the president and Congress, has made some unwise choices with the powers granted to it. This is no reason to take these powers away completely. The Republican Right is trying to do with judicial review what they are trying to do with the filibuster. They claim that these powers support tyranny, but the truth is they don't want them interfering with their own agendas.

The extreme right-wingers have described Supreme Court justices as having "typical activist flair" since the 1960s. When Justice Earl Warren struck down racist doctrines like "separate but equal" with the power of judicial review, the John Birch Society put up billboards calling for his impeachment. Even Eisenhower called his appointment "the biggest damned-fool mistake I ever made." But despite his personal feelings, Eisenhower properly used the power of the National Guard to enforce Warren's orders on school desegregation.

If Strom Thurmond had been elected president, as Senator Trent Lott opined, perhaps "all of these problems" wouldn't have happened. But Eisenhower abided by the Court, and America can be thankful that he did. No other body but the Supreme Court would have been able to erase the racist stains of segregation with such efficiency.

The Warren Court struck down "separate but equal" laws because they violated the constitutional right to "equal protection of the laws." This right was guaranteed under the Fourteenth Amendment, but for almost a century, too many Americans ignored it. Warren used the power of law to force the times to catch up to the words.

If Earl Warren had simply relied on historical research to discover the "original intent" of those who drafted Fourteenth Amendment, he may not have come to the conclusion that he did. The original intent of many of the men who passed the amendment was that equality was fine, so long as blacks kept their equality in separate quarters from whites. The Supreme Court affirmed this widespread and racist mentality in its 1896 ruling in *Plessy v. Ferguson*.

Warren knew that the Constitution was a living document, and he followed the advice of John Marshall, who said the Constitution was "intended to endure for ages to come, and, consequently, to be adapted to the various crises of human affairs." By looking at the Constitution through the lens of the present, Warren brought the words "equal protection of the laws" to its full meaning.

"We are in the age in which not only judges, not only lawyers, but even schoolchildren have come to learn that the Constitution changes," said Justice Antonin Scalia in a speech last March. "I have grammar school students come into the court now and then, and they recite very proudly what they have been taught, 'The Constitution is a living document,' *and worse.*"—That's right. *And worse.*

Maybe he would rather have David Barton teach the schoolchildren, because Scalia reads the Constitution as dogmatically as Tom DeLay reads the Old Testament. Since the words "judicial review" and "separation between church and state" don't appear word for word in the Constitution, Scalia questions their existence altogether. Joined by Justice Clarence Thomas, Scalia says he wants to revert America to what the founders "originally intended." I suggest he read *The Federalist Papers*, essay 14, wherein Madison wrote, "Is it not the glory of the people of America that... they have not suffered a blind veneration for antiquity to overrule the suggestion of their own good sense?

By positioning themselves as seekers of the true wisdom of our founding fathers, these two follow a position of "arrogance cloaked as humility," as Justice William Brennan Jr. described. "Their goal is not to venerate dead framers," said constitutional scholar Mark Tushnet, "but to restrain living judges from imposing their own values."

Denying a "Living Constitution," Thomas and Scalia deal a deathblow to the "original intents" of our founding fathers. Ranting against the powers of "activist judges" and raving against the misuse of judicial review, Scalia and Thomas hide the fact that they are just as "activist" as Earl Warren ever was. The Rehnquist Court *has struck down more federal laws than any other*

Justices Scalia and Thomas have voted to strike down congressional and state affirmative action programs, federal programs to encourage ownership of media by minorities, campaign finance reforms, various provisions of the Americans With Disabilities Act, part of the Family Medical Leave Act, state redistricting plans to increase minority representation in the state and federal legislatures, the federal Violence Against Women Act, state laws protecting the civil rights of gays, older workers, and the disabled, and land use regulations to protect people from flood damage and environmental pollution.

They want to take away abortion rights, eliminate the economic programs of the New Deal, and destroy the social programs of the Great Society. At the same time they want to boost big business. Left to the devices of Scalia and Thomas, the Fulton family would now own every ship, train, plane in America.

THANK YOU, JUSTICE SCALIA, MAY WE HAVE ANOTHER?

The theory of "original intent" assumes that the Constitution has been cryogenically frozen since its adoption in 1788. "Originalist" judges supposedly read the Constitution through the eyes of the framers. For an activity to pass constitutional muster, it must pass the three-pronged test of "original intent."

• If an activity was permitted during the time of the framers, it is constitutionally protected and any attempt to restrict it is unconstitutional.

• If an activity in question did not exist at the time of the framers, then the activity is not protected by the Constitution.

• If an activity was known to the framers and was illegal, it too can be banned without violating the Constitution. (Oops, abortion was legal back then.)

Justice Scalia, the current flag bearer on the Supreme Court for "original intent," says he will depart from these rules in one rare instance. There has to be an absolute consensus that today's society is at odds with a practice the framers permitted.

Scalia's favorite example is public flogging, an activity regularly accepted during the time of the framers but repudiated by a consensus of modern Americans. Thus, a law that banned public flogging would pass constitutional muster with Justice Scalia.

We can all be grateful for that.

TOP NINE REASONS WHY
ORIGINAL INTENT IS A FANTASY

REASON #1: WHERE DO WE START TO LOOK?

"Original" for Scalia means examining the words alone, as they would have been interpreted in 1788. Yet Robert Bork, a "strict constructionist", says we can look further, to the external documents, letters and debate to "explain" those words. Just who is right in this narrow debate? Why do these gentlemen have the ultimate answers that legal geniuses over the last two hundred plus years have missed out on?

REASON #2: ROCK, PAPER, SCISSORS

Delegates to the Constitutional Convention and the state ratifying conventions had different views with respect to different issues. Whose views were important? George Washington's?

Washington only clacked his wooden teeth once during the entire Constitutional Convention, when he spoke about an issue that has virtually no relevance to modern constitutional law: whether a congressional district should have a minimum of 30,000 or 40,000 people.

What about Thomas Jefferson? He wasn't even present at the Constitutional Convention or the ratifying convention of his home state of Virginia, as he was serving as the American diplomatic representative in France. Same for John Adams, who was serving a similar function in England.

It is impossible to say with any certainty that a consensus existed among the framers with respect to a specific issue or whose views should prevail if they disagreed about an issue. And when they did disagree, we do not know how issues were eventually decided or resolved.

REASON #3: JUST THE FACTS, MA'AM.

Nothing in the text of the Constitution requires judges to interpret the Constitution using the original intent of the Framers. James Madison was so opposed to this possibility; he refused to release his notes of the Constitutional Convention until decades after.

REASON #4: THE FOUNDERS DID NOT HAVE WIRELESS

Most of the issues that we think are important today and are being decided by judges were never even discussed by the framers. They could not have predicted that these issues would one day be decided in America's courts. These issues include euthanasia, the Internet, abortion, environmental legislation, and television.

REASON #5: WHAT DO YOU MEAN

My Alabama Dollars Ain't No Good?

Many of the issues that most preoccupied the framers' debates and are specifically addressed in the text of the Constitution are largely irrelevant or unimportant today.

Examples include: whether a presidential and vice presidential candidate can come from the same state (they can't), whether states can print their own money (they can't), whether Congress can create a standing army (it can), etc.

Even if judges knew with certainty what the framers thought, that knowledge would only be of limited utility because there is so little overlap between their constitutional world and ours.

REASON #6: NO, REALLY. INTERPRET.

The framers used broad terms to allow room for interpretation. The Fourth Amendment prohibits "unreasonable searches and seizures," but it doesn't define the term beyond that. The same is the case with the Eighth Amendment, which prohibits "cruel and unusual punishment." (Though, as Scalia notes, flogging was totally fine.)

REASON #7: CHANGE IS GOOD

The framers held certain views that are completely at odds with those of modern-day society. The most obvious example is their support or toleration of slavery. But certain framers weren't really in tune with our modern expectations of freedom of speech.

In 1798, Congress passed the Sedition Act, which outlawed virtually any criticism of the Adams administration in the press. Although the law never formally came before the Court, the Supreme Court justices at that time expressed the view that this legislation was constitutional. Maybe Scalia would approve?

REASON #8: DON'T KNOW MUCH ABOUT HISTORY

How exactly are federal judges supposed to sift through all this historical evidence? None of the sitting justices is a professional historian or has a PhD in history (Scalia's area of expertise before he became a judge was regulatory law).

REASON #9: SCALIA FLUNKED

Many professional historians of both liberal and conservative persuasions have criticized Scalia's original intent theory on the grounds that the historical analysis used by judges in implementing originalism is historically flawed and incomplete. If professional historians often cannot reach a consensus about what the framers thought about a particular issue, why does Justice Scalia think he can do better?

In the first half of the twentieth century, right-wing justices on the Supreme Court used judicial review to strike down state and federal laws that ran afoul of their extreme conservative views. They struck down a score of laws inspired by FDR's New Deal, laws that supported a minimum wage and laws that provided workplace safety.

The Court found that all these laws—enacted by democratically elected legislatures—violated constitutional rights such as "freedom of contract." These exercises in conservative judicial activism eventually came to a halt and were reversed after right-wing justices retired or died, and were replaced by FDR with mainstream justices who believed in judicial restraint.

When the extreme Right screams that the New Deal Supreme Court was a hotbed of judicial activism, they have their history completely reversed. Unlike the right-wing justices who preceded them, the New Deal justices exercised judicial restraint and upheld most of the congressional laws against the court challenges of big business and other right-wing constituencies.

CHAPTER FIFTEEN
VOX POPULI

The radical Right insists that it speaks for a disenfranchised majority of U.S. citizens, what former president Richard Nixon coined the "silent majority." Be it the Southern Baptist Convention or the American Center for Law and Justice, each and every fundamentalist and radical conservative political action committee claims to represent the mainstream beliefs of Main Street, U.S.A.

Are you "sick and tired of the leftward leanings of our government," like Senator Orrin Hatch insists we are? Millions may nod with an emphatic "Yes!" listening to Hatch on conservative radio chat shows or watching him on television. But when you consider that the country has nearly 297 million citizens, the blanket statistic "millions" is deceiving. Anything over two million will qualify.

Just to prove a point: Senator Hatch is from Utah and was elected as one of two senators in a population of millions— 2,389,039 (2004 census) people, to be exact. It's impressive that the senator has millions of constituents, but not as impressive considering that the entire population of his state is about equivalent to the city of Houston, Texas. So while the senator does speak for the "millions" in Utah, a little perspective goes a long way.

The radical Right uses this very effective method when describing its "millions" of constituents. They present their agenda as America's agenda and use generic numbers to support their claims. They are right about one thing, however, there is a silent majority of Americans—but it's not the silent majority that they would have us believe.

WHERE WE REALLY STAND

The language of politics may not have progressed much, but the science of polling is more sophisticated and accurate than ever. I realize that the framing of questions can sometimes "rig" the answers, but there are plenty of independent professionals who pride themselves on avoiding such gamesmanship. Honest opinion polls remain the single clearest indicator of what individual Americans think about national issues.

Why is polling a clear indicator? Because it relies upon a very well-known and extremely valuable discipline—STATISTICS. There are people (bless their hearts) who dedicate their lives to studying statistics and compiling infomation based on very hard data. I could give you a very large treatise on why polls are valuable and why they are reliable within a degree of error (depending upon the number of people polled), but suffice it to say that a thousand people polled can provide accuracy to plus or minus 3 percent.

Presidents as ideologically contrary as FDR and Richard Nixon regularly commissioned their own opinion polls and obsessively pored over the results. This goes on in the Bush administration as well, although President Bush has dismissed the importance of polls by saying, "If I tried to fine-tune my messages based upon polls, I think I'd be pretty ineffective." He certainly would - if success was based on promoting what the majority of Americans really believe. The president and his ultraconservative supporters don't like scientifically based polling that disputes their claims. So they ignore it and pray that the rest of us will too.

CHOICE AND CHALLENGE

Fundamentalists, and our current president, would have us believe that the abortion issue divides our country. Beloved Bush lower court nominee and former attorney general of Alabama William H. Pryor Jr. declared *Roe v. Wade*, (the U.S. Supreme Court's landmark 1973 ruling in favor of a single woman's right to choice), "the worst abomination of constitutional law in our history." Yet a January 2005 ABC News/*Washington Post* telephone poll paints a very clear picture of where the new silent majority of Americans stands on reproductive rights.

Overall, 57 percent of Americans say abortion should be legal in all or most cases. That's 193 million people nationwide. Despite all the conservative noise to the contrary, this is essentially unchanged since 1995. Of those surveyed, 21 percent said abortions should be legal in all cases and 34 percent said abortion should be legal in most cases. And 54 percent are in favor of *Roe v. Wade*.

A CNN/*USA Today*/Gallup poll conducted in July of 2005 asked 1006 randomly selected American voters, "With respect to the abortion issue, would you consider yourself to be pro-choice or pro-life?" Fifty-one percent described themselves as pro-choice, 42 percent as pro-life, 3 percent said they were "mixed/neither," 3 percent didn't know what the terms meant, and 1 percent were unsure.

That same month, CBS News did its own commemorative *Roe v. Wade* survey. "More than thirty years ago, the Supreme Court's decision in *Roe v. Wade* established a constitutional right for women to obtain legal abortions in this country," the poll began, "In general, do you think the Court's decision was a good thing or a bad thing?" Here are the results broken down by the respondents' stated political affiliation.

	Good Thing	Bad Thing	Both (vol.)	Unsure
	%	%	%	%
ALL	59	32	4	5
Republicans	47	47	1	5
Democrats	68	24	5	3
Independents	61	27	4	8

Even among Republicans, there was no majority condemning women's freedom of choice on this issue.

A Pew Research Center for the People & the Press survey in June of 2005 asked 1,464 adults, "In 1973 the *Roe v. Wade* decision established a woman's constitutional right to an abortion, at least in the first three months of pregnancy. Would you like to see the Supreme Court completely overturn its *Roe v. Wade* decision or not?" These were the results:

	Yes	No	Unsure
	%	%	%
June 2005	30	63	7
January 2003	31	62	7

The clear 2-1 margin in favor of *Roe v. Wade* doesn't appear to support any of the extreme Right's or even the Right's claim that they speak for a majority of Americans on the issue. And the numbers have barely changed since an identical poll in 2003. Broken down by gender, of those polled, 62 percent of men and 64 percent of women opposed overturning *Roe v. Wade*.

Regardless of how hard the religious Right tries to shoehorn *Roe v. Wade* into any political dialogue, Americans consistently feel the same way. The supposedly "liberal-biased media" obediently reports the radical Right's abortion stance every hour. But poll results remain the same year after year. Quinnipiac University in Connecticut polled voters in New York, New Jersey, Connecticut, Pennsylvania, and Florida over five years and compared these results:

TREND: Do you think abortion should be legal in all cases, legal in most cases, illegal in most cases, or illegal in all cases?

	Legal All	Legal Most	Illegal Most	Illegal All	DK/NA
May 25, 2005	18	37	27	14	5
Mar 10, 2005	19	35	24	15	6
Dec 15, 2004	16	41	26	13	5
Jul 24, 2004	18	35	27	13	6
May 27, 2004	20	35	26	14	6
Jun 12, 2003*	21	33	24	17	6
Mar 5, 2003	23	32	23	18	4
Mar 5, 2003*	22	32	24	18	4

The surprising reality is that despite constant political debate, unending media hype, and marches in Washington both for and against abortion rights, the issue consistently ranks low on the list of priorities cited by most voters. In a February 2004 Gallup poll, abortion ranked thirteenth, below education, the economy, the war in Iraq, health care, and immigration, among the issues most concerning Americans. It simply isn't a hot-button issue for the average voter. But it is *the* hot-budget issue for the extreme Right. And that's why it's constantly in the news.

Americans, the polls tell us, simply don't believe that women need to have their bodies and their choices regulated by pro-life politicians. Make no mistake, the issue is important to us, but to my mind these numbers say, "We'll look into our own hearts decide for ourselves." Americans, the polls tell us, simply don't believe that women need to have their bodies and their choices regulated by pro-life politicians.

LEGALLY DEAD

In March of 2005, President Bush, Governor Bush, and self-righteous lawmakers on Capitol Hill tried to hijack the federal court system. Pandering to religious extremists, these ultraconservative politicians chose to capitalize on one American family's ongoing tragedy. Countermanding a Florida court order, the president signed a bill that "would allow federal courts to hear a claim by or on behalf of Terri Schiavo for violation of her rights relating to the withholding or withdrawal of food, fluids, or medical treatment necessary to sustain her life."

As previously described, Terri Schiavo had been in a severely vegetative state for fifteen years when Terri's husband Michael made the choice to have his wife's feeding tube removed. But Terri's parents balked. They insisted that doctors continue to mechanically keep their severely brain-damaged daughter alive. The radical Right saw opportunity in the Schiavos' private tragedy and stepped right in.

The media swarmed Pinellas Park, Florida, documenting every embarrassing "devout" display by religious activists. Though strangers to Terri Schiavo, protesters felt no compunction about waving giant spoons saying "Please feed Terri," at news cameras. One pair of zealots tried to break into the hospice where Schiavo lay in order to force the virtually brain-dead woman to take Holy Communion.

The new silent majority of Americans apparently did not like what they saw. A Fox News poll on March 4, 2005 found that 59 percent of Americans would have chosen to do what Schiavo's husband did. Twenty-four percent agreed with the president and the religious Right. Seventeen percent said they weren't sure what they'd do.

Michael Schiavo contended that, were his wife physically capable of understanding the situation, she would not want her life prolonged artificially. The Fox poll found that nearly three-quarters of Americans—74 percent—would wish for their guardian to remove their own feeding tube and let nature take its course.

An ABC News poll on March 10, 2005, asked a broad selection of respondents, "If you were in this condition, would you want to be kept alive, or not?" The results completely contradicted ultraconservatives' media posturing:

	Kept Alive	Not Kept Alive	Unsure
	%	%	%
March 2005	8	87	4

On March 15, 2005, ABC polled Americans on whether Schiavo's husband or her parents were responsible for choosing her fate, and if the respondents were in Terri Schiavo's condition, whether they would want to be kept alive. This is what they found:

LIFE SUPPORT

	Spouse	Parents
Who should have final say?	65%	25%
	Yes	No
Would you want to be kept alive?	8%	87%

As the his ink dried after signing the Theresa Marie Schiavo Compromise Bill, President Bush said, "I will continue to stand on the side of those defending life for all Americans, including those with disabilities." A CNN/*USA Today* poll asked a sampling of those Americans, "Do you approve or disapprove of the way George W. Bush is handling the Terri Schiavo case?" The results reveal some question about whether a decade and a half spent brain-dead was really "disabled," as the president piously claimed.

	Approve	Disapprove	Unsure
	%	%	%
April 2005	34	53	13

The poll followed up by asking, "Do you approve or disapprove of Congress's involvement in the Terri Schiavo case?" Again, the results indicate a nation out of step with the ultra-Right's blatant grandstanding:

	Approve	Disapprove	Unsure
	%	%	%
April 2005	20	76	4

Time magazine polled respondents on the net effect of Bush's fast-and-loose jurisdictional conduct. "How about President Bush, who signed the legislation this weekend moving jurisdiction to the federal courts? Was it right for him to intervene, or not?"

	Right	Not Right	Unsure
	%	%	%
March 2005	24	70	6

Nearly three-quarters responded in defense of the Florida courts. The *Time* poll also asked, "Do you think that Congress and the president's intervention had more to do with their values and principles, or more to do with politics?"

	Value and Principles	Politics	Both (vol.)	Neither (vol.)	Unsure
	%	%	%	%	%
March 2005	25	65	4	1	5

Not surprisingly, more than six in ten respondents cried foul. Americans agreed wholeheartedly with Eleventh Circuit U.S. Court of Appeals judge Stanley F. Birch when he stopped Bush and the Right's assault on the lives of private citizens. Congress and the president "acted in a manner demonstrably at odds with our founding fathers' blueprint for the governance of a free people," Judge Birch said. The radical Right had used the federal judiciary "in a manner repugnant to the text, structure, and traditions" of our laws.

In the words of Schiavo's persecuted husband, "For Congress to come in and interfere in a personal matter is outrageous." The radical Right had compounded Michael Schiavo's personal anguish a thousandfold. Having gone through the ultraconservative wringer, he knew that their ghoulish political obsession with his private life had significance for every American. "They can do it to me, they'll do it to every person in this country," he said. "And they should be ashamed of themselves."

THE COUNTRY THAT PRAYS TOGETHER...

In his book *America Can Be Saved*, Jerry Falwell shares his vision of the future. "I hope," he writes, "that I live to see the day when, as in the early days of our country, we won't have any public schools. The churches will have taken them over and Christians will be running them."

The separation of church and state is under siege in America. Today's radical Right insists that, since the Constitution doesn't specifically prohibit prayer in public schools, then what's the harm in requiring children to pray? Whether they want to or not.

The "establishment of religion" clause in the First Amendment of the Constitution says simply this: "Congress shall make no law respecting establishment of religion." Our Constitution was drafted by lawmakers administering a new country settled by religious exiles. The establishment clause was intended to prevent the spiritual tyranny of a national religion, as existed in England. Our founding fathers wanted to keep the doctrines of faith and the ideas of politics separate from one another.

And in 1947 the Supreme Court left no doubt as to what the

establishment clause meant in a modern context. In a 5-4 decision in favor of a New Jersey state school bussing law, Justice Hugo Black defined the first clause of the First Amendment of the Bill of Rights definitively. Black wrote, "In the words of Jefferson, the clause against establishment of religion by law was intended to erect 'a wall of separation between church and state.'"

It is often difficult to decode a candidate's stance on religious issues, since no one running for office wants to be seen as antireligion. But what do Americans really believe about school prayer? Richard Mellon Scaife and other ultra-Right proponents need to puff up their extremist beliefs as "naked ideological warfare." But the new silent majority doesn't see itself on either side of Scaife's fight.

First, it's important to remember the actual religious makeup of the United States. The most recent census figures indicate that 79.8 percent of Americans describe themselves as Christian. According to a 2004 study by the National Council of the Churches of Christ in the U.S., that percentage breaks down roughly like this:

1. The Catholic Church – 67,259,768
2. Southern Baptist Convention – 16,439,603
3. The United Methodist Church – 8,251,175
4. The Church of Jesus Christ of Latter-day Saints – 5,503,192
5. The Church of God in Christ – 5,449, 875
6. National Baptist Convention, USA., Inc. – 5,000,000
7. Evangelical Lutheran Church in America – 4,984,925
8. National Baptist Convention of America, Inc. – 3,500,000
9. Presbyterian Church (USA) – 3,241,309
10. Assemblies of God – 2,729,562

America, the numbers tell us, is mostly a Christian country. Five out of six Americans say they are Christians. Catholics and Protestants comprise half the adult population (25 percent and 26 percent, respectively). Another 32 percent call themselves Christians but say they are neither Catholic nor Protestants. Almost half of Christians say they are "born-again," and one-fourth describe themselves as "evangelical Christians."

Jews and Mormons make up another 2 percent of the total. Muslims, Hindus, and Buddhists are each less than 1 percent of the population. About 3 percent claim some other religion.

Since the Far Right is always talking about the evil atheists, let's quickly look at the term. Atheism, broadly defined, is simply the absence of belief in the existence of any gods. An atheist is a person who is not a theist. Christians insist that atheism means the denial of the existence of any gods. While there are 'strong' atheists who may take this position, most seem to just have no belief whatsoever. Rather than some evil force in the world, this group is actually rather benign when it comes to religion. Agnosticism is the position that knowledge of God or gods is not possible; this group recognizes the question but can't come up with an answer for themselves.

As of 2005, according to the Barna Group, a Christian information organization that compiles religious statistics, 15 percent of adults nationwide identify themselves as having no religion, and within this group about 9 percent actually identify themselves as atheist or agnostic.

The Barna Group also says that American Christians who describe themselves as "evangelical" is holding steady at only

7 percent of the adult population. The ultra-Right may claim momentum, but Barna polls also say the number of Americans who are born-again is staying constant, not growing.

When it comes to teaching schoolchildren evolution or "intelligent design," a Christian fundamentalist buzzword for creationism, those same Americans remain fair-minded but clear. A CBS News poll in November, 2004 reported that even among those who identify themselves as Bush voters, 71 percent want evolution included in their children's education. A Harris poll in June 2005 indicates that 55 percent of Americans was creationism or intelligent design taught along with evolution. The majority of the public does not buy the notion put forward by creationists that you must choose between the Bible and evolution.

Heedless of what the majority of Americans actually believe, extreme Right religious leaders keep working to replace any judge in favor of maintaining separation between church and state. The extreme Right isn't just on the margins of American opinion, they're on the radical fringe of American religion.

The facts are clear—despite the Far Right's claims to a new moral agenda, most Americans take a very moderate stance. Religion has no place in politics. Faith, like choice, is a scrupulously guarded right Americans are proud to reserve for themselves, not surrender to their leaders.

MARRIED WITH...

"I believe marriage is between a man and a woman,
and I think we ought to codify that one way or another."
George W. Bush

When the president came out in favor of a constitutional amendment banning same-sex marriages, the *New York Times* declared it "an impassioned endorsement...after weeks of intensive lobbying by social conservatives." The gay marriage furor has generated sound bites, headlines, and unending footage of happy couples tying the knot in San Francisco and Massachusetts for more than a year. But a recent CBS News/*New York Times* poll asked, "Do you think defining marriage as a union only between a man and a woman is an important enough issue to be worth changing the Constitution for, or isn't it that kind of issue?" This is what they found:

	Important Enough	Not That Kind of Issue	Unsure
	%	%	%
April 2005	38	56	6

Simply put, the majority of Americans don't believe that legally recognizing citizens' lifestyle choices needs to be blocked at a constitutional level. Once again, the new silent majority of Americans just doesn't think it's an issue. William Pryor may believe that same-sex couples belong in prison, but most Americans don't think homosexuality is a crime.

A *USA Today* poll from October of 2003 concluded that any lingering discomfort about gay unions was merely a generational hangover. Of those surveyed, 67 percent of respondents ages eighteen to twenty-nine and 53 percent of those ages thirty to forty-nine said gay unions would have no harmful effect or might make society better.

Similarly, the American Enterprise Institute, a conservative think tank, discovered that public acceptance of gays in the military has grown from 51 percent in a 1977 Gallup poll to 80 percent in 2003. Citing surveys indicating that about 60 percent of Americans now believe that homosexual relations between consenting adults should be legal, up from just over 40 percent in the mid-1970s, the Enterprise Institute's Karlyn Bowman concluded that "society is certainly changing its mind" on same-sex relationships.

THE GUNS OF WASHINGTON

During the 2002 suburban D.C. sniper attacks, White House spokesman Ari Fleisher responded to a gun control question with a question of his own: "How many laws can we really have to stop crime, if people are determined in their heart to violate them no matter how many there are or what they say?"

Right-wing extremists have long argued that their right to own and carry any and all guns is guaranteed under the Second Amendment to the Constitution. They claim that Congress doesn't have the right to enact gun controls of any kind. Fortunately, since 1939, the Supreme Court has seen it differently. As the extreme Right takes aim at vacant seats on the federal bench, it's only a matter of time before Congress's right to pass gun legislation is once again tested in the highest court.

But in poll after poll, the new silent majority of Americans clearly sees gun control as an area where the government should actually get more involved. The majority of Americans oppose the extreme Right's position on guns. Americans staunchly advocate stricter gun control laws, and they have for years.

A 2000 CNN poll found that six in ten Americans believe that laws covering the sale of firearms should be more stringent than they are now. And a Gallup poll conducted four years later shows that most Americans continue to feel that guns need to be difficult to buy. "In general," the Gallup pollsters asked, "do you feel that the laws covering the sale of firearms should be made more strict, less strict, or kept as they are now?"

	More Strict	Less Strict	Kept As Now	No Opinion
	%	%	%	%
October 2004	54	11	34	1

And after NRA-supported Republican lawmakers allowed the 1994 assault rifle ban to expire in 2004, an NBC/*Wall Street Journal* poll gauged America's response. "Overall," the poll asked, "are you satisfied that this law has expired, dissatisfied that it has expired, or does it not make a difference to you either way?"

	%
Satisfied	12
Dissatisfied	61
No difference	25
Not sure	2

Apparently, the average American isn't as eager to own an assault rifle as radical right-wing lawmakers would like. Nor is the average Republican voter—a Harris poll asked Democrats, Republicans, and Independents if they favored the assault rifle ban.

	Favor	Oppose	Unsure
	%	%	%
ALL	71	26	4
Republicans	72	25	3
Democrats	72	27	1
Independents	74	22	3

And, as is uniformly the case with most crucial issues on the radical Right's agenda, Americans' opposition to the ultraconservative position on the gun issue has remained consistent. A series of Harris polls asked, "In general, would you say you favor stricter gun control or less strict gun control?"

	Stricter	Less Strict	Neither (vol.)	Unsure
	%	%	%	%
September 2004	60	32	4	3
May 2000	63	28	6	4
June 1999	63	25	10	2
April 1998	69	23	7	1

A recent Gallup poll found that "nearly two in three Americans say they would feel less safe if they were in a public place and knew that concealed firearms were allowed." Of gun owners themselves, 45 percent said they would feel less safe in a place where concealed firearms were permitted.

STEM CELL PARALYSIS

When George Bush issued his 2001 condemnation of federal funding for stem-cell research, the scientific community was shocked. But as the possible benefits of harvesting and researching human embryonic stem cells became more widely understood by the public, the new silent majority of Americans rejected the extreme Right's parochial position.

If it means a cure for spinal cord injuries, Alzheimer's, and other brain and nerve diseases, isn't it at least worth exploring? The majority of Americans, led by Nancy Reagan, say yes. A *Wall Street Journal* poll conducted just before Bush's announcement found that 72 percent of Roman Catholics questioned were in favor of the research their church itself rejects on moral grounds. On this issue, the Right doesn't have a prayer of support from average Americans.

Even though Bush and the proselytizing ultraconservatives continue to oppose federally funding stem-cell research, one by one hard-line, radical Republican senators like Robert Bennett, Orrin Hatch, and Trent Lott all asked the president to reconsider. Tommy Thompson, Bush's former Health and Human Services secretary and a staunch pro-lifer, has even weighed in on the side of funding research. And in August of 2005, Bill Frist, anti-abortion MD and the radical Right's attack dog on Capitol Hill, finally came out against President Bush's faith-based position. "It's not just a matter of faith," Frist declared before the Senate, "it's a matter of science."

American opinion has stayed consistent for half a decade. The Barna Group found that the new silent majority supports funding research by a two to one margin, and this was before many of Capitol Hill's most prominent conservatives began to do an about-face on the issue. In July of 2005, CBS News asked, "Do you approve or disapprove of medical research using embryonic stem cells?" The response, organized by stated political party, looked like this:

	Approve	Disapprove	Unsure
	%	%	%
ALL	56	30	14
Republicans	46	42	12
Democrats	60	29	11
Independents	60	21	19

After California's Governor Schwarzenegger broke from the conservative pack and supported a California state referendum in favor of stem-cell research, *Time* magazine posed this question in May, 2005: "Last fall, California voters approved raising $3 billion in state money for stem-cell research, including developing more lines of embryonic stem cells. Do you personally agree more with:

	% WHO AGREE
"The president's decision to restrict federally funded embryonic stem-cell research"	20
"Californians who voted to fund additional stem-cell research"	50
"Government funds shouldn't be used for this type of stem-cell research at all"	22
Unsure	8

Time followed up by asking, "Should other states follow California's lead in funding all types of stem-cell research, or not?"

	Should	Should Not	Unsure
	%	%	%
May 2005	53	37	9

From ABC News/*Washington Post* this year (63 percent in favor of embryonic stem-cell research) to Fox News in 2003, (46 percent in favor of embryonic tissue research, 37 percent against, and 17 percent unsure) the overwhelming majority of Americans adamantly support exploring this promising new field of medical research. Ultraconservative Roman Catholic and Protestant religious leaders agree that stem-cell research is immoral. The majority of their followers don't.

YOU HAVE THE RIGHT TO REMAIN DEAD

In the 1980s, Judge John Roberts, then just a lawyer for Ronald Reagan's Justice Department, urged the high court to streamline its caseload by "abdicating the role of fourth or fifth guesser in death penalty cases." Roberts also wrote that the federal court of appeals' willingness to hear state prisoners' death penalty cases, "goes far to making a mockery of the entire criminal justice system." But the moderate majority of Americans don't see it that way.

Though the religious Right swears by capital punishment, average Americans are opposed to state-sanctioned execution. A CBS News opinion poll conducted in April of 2005 asked, "What do you think should be the penalty for persons convicted of murder—the death penalty, life in prison with no chance of parole, or a long prison sentence with a chance of parole?" Only 39 percent of the respondents chose the death penalty; 39 percent chose life with no parole, 6 percent said a long sentence with parole, and 13 percent volunteered the answer "Depends."

To death penalty advocates, execution is an ideal deterrent to violent crime. But most Americans disagree. A Gallup poll conducted from May 2–4, 2004, asked a broad sample of American voters, "Do you feel that the death penalty acts as a deterrent to the commitment of murder, that it lowers the murder rate, or not?" The results, when stacked on top of results from an identical poll done in 1991, reveal a growing distrust in the hangman:

	Does Deter	Does Not	No Opinion
	%	%	%
May 2004	35	62	3
June 1991	51	41	8

Americans, it seems, have checked the facts. Similarly, a 2003 Harris poll asked, "Do you feel that executing people who commit murder deters others from committing murder, or do you think such executions don't have much effect?" The Harris results were also compared to previous polls since 1976. This is what they found:

	Deters Others	Not Much Effect	Not Sure
	%	%	%
2003	41	53	6
2001	42	52	7
2000	44	50	7
1999	47	49	4
1997	49	49	2
1983	63	32	5
1976	59	34	7

These results indicate a clear shift from relying on execution to prevent crime to doubting its effectiveness. The Harris poll also asked, "Do you think that innocent people are sometimes convicted of murder or that this never happens?" These results, the numbers tell us, have remained consistent for more than a decade:

	Some-times	Never	Not Sure
	%	%	%
2003	95	4	2
2001	94	3	3
2000	94	5	1
1999	95	3	1

Apparently the new silent majority agrees with Supreme Court justice John Paul Stevens. Speaking at an American Bar Association meeting in August of 2005, Stevens said the advent of DNA evidence has revealed that "a substantial number of death sentences have been imposed erroneously." Regardless of the extreme Right's claims to the contrary, the new silent majority of Americans simply does not believe that the death penalty is an acceptable form of punishment.

CHAPTER SIXTEEN
THE NUCLEAR OPTION

On February 26, 2003, Ted Stevens, the sixty-nine-year-old, six-term Republican senator from Alaska, sat on a wooden chair in a Senate cloakroom. He wore a tie with a drawing of the Incredible Hulk, the gigantic, green comic-book hero. Stevens was angry; Democrats had used the filibuster to block yet another of President Bush's judicial nominees. As other senators and aides listened, Stevens fumed, "We can put an end to this now! "

He outlined a procedural maneuver that would end the Democrats' ability to filibuster judicial nominees. Excited aides named the strategy the "Hulk" in honor of Stevens's tie. If exercised, it could render the filibuster obsolete in any context, fundamentally altering the nature of the Senate. In the following months Stevens and his supporters couldn't find much support, even among other Republicans, for using the "Hulk."

Meanwhile, the war over Bush's judicial nominees intensified. Now that the 2002 elections had once again given Republicans a majority, GOP senators changed Judiciary Committee rules to ensure that Democrats could not keep Bush's nominees from going to the full Senate for a vote. The president resubmitted the nomination of Charles Pickering, a judge that Democrats had rejected the year before when they controlled the Senate.

Left with no other way to stop him, the Democrats filibustered Pickering's nomination and then stalled another nominee, Miguel Estrada, as well. GOP Senate staffers took advantage of a computer glitch to monitor Democratic files (their bosses claimed to be "mortified") and discovered that the Democrats planned additional filibusters if necessary. Conservative senators began seriously discussing the use of the "Hulk"—and rechristened it the "nuclear option."

Some people wondered why they were working themselves into such a lather. The Republicans had routinely obstructed judicial nominees during the Clinton years, even using the filibuster on a couple of occasions. Moreover, the federal courts were already solidly Republican. Six of the nine Supreme Court justices had been nominated by a Republican president, and Republican appointees controlled ten of the thirteen federal courts of appeal. If they already controlled the courts, why did the GOP suddenly care so much about just a few appointees?

The answer: ultraconservative Senate Republicans and activists on the religious Right don't just want mainstream Republican judges. They want "strict constructionists," reactionary jurists who will clear the last obstacle to the evangelical agenda—the independent judiciary. And in 2003, with a conservative evangelical in the White House, they had a chance to realize their goal. But Bush's re-election was far from a sure thing—the extreme Right knew it had to force its nominees through quickly. Democrats knew it too, and so they used the filibuster.

On November 12, 2003, thirty hard-line senators marched into the body's chamber for an overnight "talkathon"—complete with cots and other props—to demand votes on all of Bush's judicial nominees. Jon Kyl of Arizona sternly intoned, "It is a solemn responsibility of the Senate to act on the president's nominees. We are not fulfilling that responsibility." Democrats accused Republicans of "whining" and "crying" and dismissed the stunt as a "colossal waste of time."

It was, but it hinted at a much more serious confrontation to come. The fight over the filibuster had just begun.

ESCALATIONS

The Senate is a distinctively American legislative body. With two members from each state regardless of the size of a state's population, it embodies the principle that the minority will be given a voice. The Senate's procedural rules, though arcane, have developed over time with this central purpose in mind: to encourage deliberation and compromise by making it harder for the majority to run roughshod over those who disagree with it. According to James Madison, "The use of the Senate is to consist in proceeding with more coolness, with more system, and with more wisdom, than the popular branch."

Made famous by movies like *Mr. Smith Goes to Washington*, the filibuster is only the most well-known of these rules. It allows a senator or group of senators to prolong debate indefinitely, thereby holding a bill (or judicial nomination) hostage by preventing it from ever coming to a vote (the term "filibuster" derives from the Dutch word for "pirate").

Because of this threat, the party controlling the Senate has generally been careful not to provoke its use by the minority. Customs emerged over time to assure the minority a certain degree of leverage. This leverage, in turn, ensured a degree of moderation in the Senate's decisions—including the confirmation of federal judges.

But when President Bush took office in 2001, conservative Republicans, suddenly in control of both the executive and legislative branches, had no interest in moderation. They used various strategies to limit Democratic influence over the judicial selection process. President Bush chose not to consult with the Judiciary Committee when selecting nominees to the federal courts. President Clinton had always done so.

In February 2003, committee Democrats did not feel that they had been given enough time to consider two appellate court nominees. A Senate rule says that at least one minority member has to agree before discussion of a matter can be ended. But when the senators tried to invoke the rule, Orrin Hatch, the chairman of the Judiciary Committee, forced a vote on the nominees anyway.

Three months later, a Democratic member of the committee, Senator Charles Schumer, questioned current Supreme Court nominee John Roberts, then being considered for a seat on a federal appeals court. Hatch lost patience with Schumer's queries. "Some, I think are dumb-ass questions," he carped. "I feel badly saying it, between you and me, but I do know dumb-ass questions when I see dumb-ass questions."

Republicans have repeatedly contended that Senate tradition, if not the Constitution itself, requires that each judicial nominee get an up-or-down vote by the full Senate. The claim is blatantly hypocritical—during Clinton's presidency they repeatedly bowed to demands from extremist conservatives ("no more Clinton judges!") to simply deny votes to over fifty of the president's nominees.

To do so they employed a variety of back-room strategies—strategies they later denied to the Democrats. One of these, called the "hold," allowed just one senator to stall a nomination—and the senator could do it anonymously. In 1999, Hatch, who is from Utah, shut the entire confirmation process down until Clinton nominated a Utah Republican to the bench.

Most common was the "blue slip." During Clinton's presidency Hatch enforced this policy, which says that a nomination cannot go forward until both senators from a nominee's home state return a "blue slip" to the Judiciary Committee. Senators stopped nominees by simply not returning the slip.

But when Bush became president and Hatch regained the chairmanship, he suddenly changed the rule. The blue slips, he said, were just advisory—Bush's nominees could move forward without them.

Despite their recent lapses of memory, in a couple of cases where they found Clinton nominees particularly odious, Republicans even resorted to the filibuster! Senator Frist, on the front lines threatening to eliminate this tactic, was also out front when he helped to filibuster a Clinton nominee—Judge Richard A. Paez.

The "nuclear option" crisis, in other words, did not come about because Democrats abused the filibuster. It happened because conservative Senate Republicans, egged on by extremist evangelicals, intentionally upset the Senate's delicate balance of power and sought to shut out Democrats from the process for selecting federal judges altogether.

In most cases Republican gamesmanship wasn't even necessary—the vast majority of Bush's judicial nominees were confirmed, without denying the Democrats their input. By the summer of 2005, the Senate had confirmed 92 percent of Bush's judicial nominees, compared with 84 percent of Clinton's.

But in a few instances where Bush-nominated judges were far to the right of the legal mainstream and his party closed off all other methods of objecting, Democrats felt it necessary to use their last remaining weapon. It proved effective. Republicans controlled the Senate, but barely, and had much less than the sixty votes necessary to stop a filibuster. The Republicans tried six times to force a vote on Estrada and twice to stop a filibuster on another nominee, Priscilla Owen. All the attempts failed.

When Congress adjourned at the end of 2003, a frustrated President Bush used his constitutional power to make "recess appointments" (temporary appointments which do not require congressional approval) to place two of these nominees, Charles Pickering and William Pryor, on the bench.

Democrats responded to this infrequently used tactic with more filibusters; in 2004 they blocked ten nominations. Republicans fumed that the stalls violated a Senate tradition (apparently newly discovered) that filibusters against a nominee with majority support in the full Senate were not allowed. *Can you believe what the Democrats are doing?* But what alternative did they have? To roll over and play dead?

In any case, Republicans now found themselves in a difficult position. Frustrated by Democratic determination on the left, they were forced to keep upping the ante by increasingly hysterical rhetoric from their right-wing supporters. James Dobson called the confrontation over judges the "most important issue that has come before the Senate since World War II," a "collision between right and wrong and good and evil. "

Giving in to this pressure, Senate Republicans began to talk, at first somewhat hesitantly, about Stevens's "nuclear option," a series of procedural steps that would reduce the votes necessary to end a filibuster from sixty to fifty-one. The Democrats were powerless to resist this maneuver—they simply did not have the votes.

The "option" is "nuclear" because it would alter the basic functioning of the Senate as a deliberative body. In the nineteenth century only the unanimous consent of the Senate could end a filibuster. Over time, senators lowered this threshold, first to sixty-seven and then, in 1975, to sixty. Moving the threshold to fifty-one, though, effectively eliminates the filibuster altogether in today's political climate.

Republicans said they would only "go nuclear" on judicial nominees. But custom and precedent matter in the Senate. Once Republicans set the example, the majority party would likely have few qualms about using the nuclear option to stop filibusters on almost any type of matter. More to the point, legislative matters can always be repealed down the road, but a lifetime judicial appointment cannot. Is it really so unreasonable to want at least sixty out of a hundred U.S. senators to concur on the character and quality of a federal judge who may serve for decades?

But the Senate would also become free to confirm even the

most extreme judicial nominees, and to evangelicals that's all that really mattered. As the 2004 elections approached, with time possibly running out on Bush's presidency, their question to Senate Republicans became more and more insistent—*what are you waiting for!?!*

Ultraconservatives argued that they had to use the nuclear option to stop the abuse of the filibuster by Democrats. According to them, the battle was just part of the overall struggle to restore their constitutional order, where senators don't abuse the filibuster and judges don't legislate from the bench.

But for the religious Right, at least, that justification was the thinnest of pretexts. The nuclear option, along with other methods advocated by evangelicals and reactionaries to control the judiciary, are not good-hearted efforts to force out-of-control judges to play their proper constitutional role. They are attempts to remove judges as an obstacle to an extremist agenda of social control.

In the 2004 elections, Republicans won a clear majority in the Senate. They now hold fifty-five of that body's seats—and were dominated by ultraconservatives. Six of the seven Republican freshmen have served previously in the House, where the majority's sway is complete, and have little patience for so-called Senate tradition. Most are more conservative than their senior colleagues, and they strongly supported use of the nuclear option.

President Bush won re-election only narrowly, but he and his supporters have asserted a mandate nevertheless. In February of this year, the president resubmitted the judicial nominees that Democrats had rejected in his first term. Both Bush and the religious Right knew that the nominations guaranteed new filibusters—and the showdown in the Senate for which they had been waiting.

Their hour had come at last. Extremist evangelicals began banging the drum to create a sense of crisis—and keep the pressure on Senate Republicans. On ABC's *This Week*, George Stephanopoulos asked Pat Robertson the following question:

> **But, sir, you have described this in pretty, this whole battle in pretty apocalyptic terms. You've said that liberals are engaged in an all-out assault on Christianity, that Democrats will appoint judges who don't share our Christian values and will dismantle Christian culture, and that the out-of-control judiciary, and this was in your last book Courting Disaster, is the most serious threat America has faced in nearly four hundred years of history, more serious than Al Qaeda, more serious than Nazi Germany and Japan, more serious than the Civil War?**

Robertson's answer: "George, I really believe that."

On April 24, 2005, evangelicals staged their first *Justice Sunday*, a satellite telecast in which Dobson and others railed against the federal judiciary as "unelected and unaccountable and arrogant and imperious and…out of control." Back in Washington, Senate majority leader Bill Frist, needing the support of the extreme Right in the event he decided to run for president, marshaled his Senate troops.

Multimillion-dollar ad campaigns arguing both sides of the

debate filled the airwaves. Reactionary ads tried to convince Americans that because of the Democrats, "courtrooms sit empty, while thousands of Americans have their cases delayed… Enough is enough."

In fact, the number of vacancies in the federal courts had gone down since Bush's presidency began. And most courtrooms sat empty not because of filibusters but because of Bush's failure to make nominations. As of May 2005, forty-six federal judgeships were vacant, but Bush had named only sixteen nominees for those slots.

Finally, on Wednesday, May 18, as a rally took place on the steps of the Capitol, Frist stood in the Senate and said, "I do not rise for party, I rise for principle." The majority leader did not mention that he had supported the filibuster against that Clinton judicial nominee in 2000.

Frist set a deadline—if the two sides did not reach a truce by Tuesday, May 24, he would exercise the nuclear option. As a heated debate proceeded in the Senate, Republicans sacrificed their own credibility to score political points. Senator Gordon Smith, a Republican from Oregon, said that Democrats sought to "bar the door to judicial service to people of faith," conveniently ignoring the fact that many of the judges condemned by ultraconservatives— including George Greer and Anthony Kennedy—are serious Christians themselves. In fact, I am unable to name *any* judges on federal or state benches who are not persons of the Christian faith.

The speeches continued over the weekend of May 21 and 22. Attempts to negotiate a compromise faltered, and Frist's deadline approached. The majority leader's staff held a conference call never back down.

By May 23, 2005, five days of debate in the Senate proved fruitless. Frist's deadline, after which he had vowed to exercise the nuclear option, would expire the following day. In the evening, workers at the Capitol again brought in cots for an overnight debate. Democrats and Republicans planned rival showings of *Mr. Smith Goes to Washington* to galvanize their supporters (both sides laid claim to Jimmy Stewart). Tony Perkins's Family Research Council issued a press release warning Republicans that "concession is not an option."

In an office away from the chamber, fourteen senators, seven Democrats and seven Republicans, continued working toward a compromise. Robert Byrd of West Virginia, with forty-four years' experience in the Senate, prodded his colleagues at the start of each gathering with the words "country, institution, then us."

On the night of the twenty-third they finally emerged with a deal. The seven Democrats agreed that three of Bush's nominees could be voted on and said they would filibuster new judicial nominees only in "extraordinary circumstances." In return, the seven Republicans agreed not to support the nuclear option.

"I say thank God, thank God, for this moment and these colleagues of mine," exulted Byrd. Lindsey Graham of South Carolina, a Republican, said, "We've got a chance to start over, and we better take it."

But Republicans who didn't participate in the deal took a different view. The compromise meant that all but two of Bush's pending nominees would get through, but still it wasn't enough.

"A major disappointment," said George Allen of Virginia. Trent Lott vowed that ultraconservatives would pick apart the deal.

And evangelicals howled. The deal was a "devil's bargain," a "betrayal of democracy, decency, and fairness," a "complete capitulation." Rick Scarborough, the chairman of the Judeo-Christian Council for Constitutional Restoration, said he had "rarely been more sickened than I am at this moment." Dobson promised that "voters will remember both Democrats and Republicans who betrayed their trust."

One wonders if Democrats should be the ones lamenting the compromise. In a visit to Pat Robertson's *700 Club* two days after the deal, Frist made it clear that if Democrats filibuster a nominee under what he deems less than "extraordinary circumstances," he will use the nuclear option. "I'm going to pull it out and I'm going to take it to the floor, and we're going to get an up-or-down vote."

Ultraconservatives seem unable, or unwilling, to imagine that the nuclear option might one day be turned against them by the Democrats—that they might reap what they have sown. In the meantime, their willingness to use this destructive tactic may well convince Democrats not to filibuster any more judicial nominees. Doing so would again risk the future of the Senate as a deliberative body devoted to compromise and moderation. For now, Republicans hold the clear upper hand.

. And the assault on that other force for moderation—the independent judiciary—continues. Janice Rogers Brown is now a judge on the federal appeals court, as is Priscilla Owen. At least until the next presidential election, additional hard-right nominees are sure to follow.

Evangelical conservatives fervently hope to make the debate over the nuclear option irrelevant. Focusing on "soft" Democratic Senate seats (and moderate Republicans as well) in the upcoming elections, they hope to capture a sufficient number to override any future filibuster by the Democrats, whether it relates to judicial nominees or not.

Additionally, with "their" judges permitting the Republicans to reshape congressional districts at will, current and future victories in the state and national legislatures will lock up their hold on this branch of government.

Then truly nothing will stand in their way.

CHAPTER SEVENTEEN
FREEDOM UNDER FIRE

On a winter evening in New Mexico, several hundred church members gather around a bonfire to burn Harry Potter books. "Witchcraft is real," says their minister, who calls the books masterpieces of "satanic deception."

In Aiken, South Carolina, a pastor exhorts his congregation to throw "anything unpleasing to God" into the fire. Up in smoke go a DVD of *Titanic*, some Bud Light cans, and a pack of playing cards.

In Pennsylvania a congregation circles around another fire. Into the flames go Bruce Springsteen CDs, the Disney cartoon *Pinocchio*, Mormon religious books, and a coconut carved with the face of a pink pig.

What, you may ask, is the problem with all this? People have the right to burn books, don't they? Absolutely. The problem is not that people burn their own books—it's that they want to burn yours too. Earlier this year, an Alabama legislator proposed banning literature by gay authors or about gay characters— Truman Capote, W.H. Auden, and Shakespeare included.

Censorship, unfortunately, is only the beginning. In a 1987 book, George Grant, a former official of Coral Ridge Ministries, wrote, "Christian politics has as its primary intent the conquest of the land—of men, families, institutions, bureaucracies, courts and governments for the Kingdom of Christ." Gary North, a Christian Reconstructionist, talks about training a generation of children in Christian schools who would grow up to construct "a Bible-based social, political and religious order which finally denies the religious liberty of the enemies of God."

One argues with fanatics in vain, but we must remember the precious thing they threaten. The extreme religious Right wants to take away your freedom to make your own moral choices. It is pushing its agenda in every part of our society: schools, churches, legislatures—and the courts. Judges will either enforce their program or the courts themselves must be destroyed.

As for what you are allowed to read, many local school boards are acutally editing their libraries, but few judges are likely to permit substantial censorship any time soon. Government-sponsored book burnings, at least for now, seem a remote possibility. But in a number of other areas, the battle over the federal judiciary will have profound significance in the coming years.

Will the courts be a bulwark against oppression or an instrument of it? Will they allow the religious Right to make the most important decisions of your life for you, from the workplace to the bedroom, from birth to death?

SEXUALITY

A little after 10:00 p.m. on September 17, 1998, Roger David Nance called the sheriff's office in Houston, Texas, to report a disturbance. A man in the apartment next door, Nance said, had a gun and was "going crazy." Officers rushed to the scene. Sheriff's deputy Joseph Quinn drew his pistol and entered through the apartment's unlocked door.

Inside he found not an angry man with a gun but two men, medical technologist John Lawrence and street-stand barbecue vendor Tyron Garner, having sex. Quinn did what any law-enforcing Texas deputy would: he arrested them. (Neighbor Nance, who had been harassing the two men, later admitted that he had lied about the "disturbance" and served fifteen days in jail.)

Garner called the arrest "sort of Gestapo," but Quinn was really just doing his job. Texas law prohibited "deviate sexual intercourse with another individual of the same sex." Both Lawrence and Garner paid $200 fines and spent the night in jail.

During the night, the two men asked themselves a question: why should consensual sex between two adults in the privacy of their own home be illegal? They sued, challenging the Texas law as unconstitutional.

Observers said they had little chance of winning. Sixteen years earlier, a Georgia man named Michael Hardwick had asked the Supreme Court to invalidate a similar Georgia law in Georgia. The Court's response, by a 5-4 vote: "This we are quite unwilling to do." Based on this precedent, the Texas appeals court upheld the convictions of Lawrence and Garner.

Ultraconservatives breathed a sigh of relief; homosexuality rouses passions on the extreme Right that are difficult to overstate. Jerry Falwell's own words illustrate: "These perverted homosexuals...absolutely hate everything that you and I and most decent, God-fearing citizens stand for...Make no mistake.

These deviants seek no less than total control and influence in society, politics, our schools, and in our exercise of free speech and religious freedom…If we do not act now, homosexuals will own America!" (They will have to topple the *Fortune 500* first.)

Despite these apocalyptic blusterings, the Supreme Court agreed to hear Lawrence and Garner's case. A lively oral argument took place on March 26, 2003. Discussion centered on the state's justification for the law. The High Court will uphold laws that discriminate against certain groups so long as the law has a "rational basis" that furthers a "legitimate state interest."

Charles Rosenthal, the counsel for Texas, struggled to articulate how Lawrence and Garner's conduct had harmed a "legitimate state interest"—or how they had hurt anyone at all. He fell back on the argument—often employed by ultraconservatives—that homosexual conduct is "immoral."

Justice Breyer noted the danger in this reasoning, pointing out that during World War I people considered it immoral to teach German in schools.

"There is a rational basis," insisted Rosenthal—declining to state what it was.

"You're not giving us a rational basis," Breyer pointed out.

Here Justice Scalia interjected: "The rational basis is that the state thinks it's immoral. Like bigamy or adultery."

"Or teaching German," remarked Breyer.

That settled things. In a landmark ruling, the Court voted 6-3 to invalidate Texas's law against sodomy. Justice Kennedy held that "The petitioners are entitled to respect for their private lives. The State cannot demean their existence or control their destiny by making their private sexual conduct a crime."

Scalia fumed that the Court had signed on to the "homosexual agenda," but gay rights supporters hailed *Lawrence v. Texas* as a landmark, a *Brown v. Board of Education* for homosexuals. Actually, it was only a small step. The decision merely gave adult gays the right to have intimate relations in privacy—it neither protected them from discrimination at work nor gave them the right to marriage or even civil unions. Those battles remain to be fought.

And they will not be easy. Speaking of gay marriage, ultraconservatives say that they "have never seen anything that has energized and provoked our grass roots like this issue, including *Roe v. Wade*." President Bush supports a constitutional amendment banning gay marriage, and in the November 2004 elections, eleven states approved bans of their own.

Some courts have ruled such prohibitions unconstitutional, so again, reactionaries are trying to take courts out of the equation altogether. In 2004 the U.S. House of Representatives passed a measure that would have stripped the courts of the ability to hear challenges to the federal Defense of Marriage Act. The bill has been reintroduced this year. As one Democratic representative has said, "Republicans have decided that if you are gay, you should be able to get along with just two branches of government."

Precisely. To reactionaries, *Lawrence v. Texas* demonstrates conclusively judges' determination to "impose their personal views on the rest of us," according to Mark Levin, author of *Men in Black: How the Supreme Court is Destroying America.* This is utter nonsense—it is ultraconservatives who want to impose *their* personal views on homosexuals and those people who openly support or merely tolerate the gay community. The six majority justices in the *Lawrence* case are not imposing anything on anyone. They simply disallowed the jailing of two adults for engaging in consensual sexual conduct. Despite the constant refrain that "courts are giving 'special rights' to gays," actually judges are simply ensuring that this minority has the *same* rights as other American citizens.

And their disapproval, of course, doesn't stop with homosexuality—it extends to any sex outside of marriage.

If you're in the bedroom with anyone other than your opposite-sex spouse, stop what you're doing. You don't get to choose.

WORK

Homosexuals do face discrimination at work—and in most places it is perfectly legal. Currently only sixteen states prohibit employers from discriminating based on sexual orientation, and no federal laws specifically prohibit it.

The extreme Right still says that discrimination against gays is okay because they are "not an economically disadvantaged people" and homosexuality is not "an immutable characteristic"— probably news to a lot of gay people.

Homosexuals, of course, are not the only ones who face workplace discrimination. The vast majority of discrimination claims are based on race and sex. Ultraconservatives oppose many of these claims as well. Why?

One of the curious things about the religious Right is its hostility to the disadvantaged and its blind worship of the free market. Opposed to welfare and the minimum wage, the movement believes that companies should be allowed to do business without interference from the government. It therefore opposes laws against employment discrimination—and fights to limit them whenever it can.

In many, if not most, discrimination cases, the victim can't prove that the employer intended to discriminate—employers generally don't make that mistake anymore. As a result, federal law and decades of Supreme Court precedent allow claims based on disparate impact. Under this theory, victims can recover if they show that an employer's practices clearly disfavor a particular group and that no good business reason exists for the practice.

In 1971, a group of African-Americans sued their employer, Duke Power Company. Before promoting employees to higher-paying departments, Duke Power required that they have a high school diploma and pass two aptitude tests. Even though the policy did not discriminate against anyone on its face, it blocked promotion for a larger number of blacks. The company failed to prove that the policy had anything to do with the ability of employees to perform the higher-paying jobs. If there was a legitimate justification, the policy would appropriately have passed muster. The Court held that the policy merely safeguarded Duke Power's practice of preferring whites.

For the record, I have written extensively about this subject in *The Case Against Lawyers*. I do not want relevant standards lowered to, for example, admit more women firefighters or disabled doctors if they cannot do the actual work necessary for these jobs. But if they are capable, then unnecessary barriers designed solely to keep certain groups out of the workforce should come down.

Ultraconservatives strongly oppose the disparate impact theory. A conservative Washington legal group says the doctrine should "be attacked at every opportunity." And federal courts have limited workers' protections against discrimination in a number of ways.

Most federal appeals courts have ruled that disparate impact claims are not even allowed to prove age discrimination—if you believe that you were discriminated against because of age, then you must specifically prove that the employer intended to fire *you* because of your age. Employers just have to hide their goals—not a very difficult thing to do—and they can do whatever they want. This is exactly how ultraconservatives, who favor corporate over individual interests, like it.

President Bush's extreme judicial nominees would roll back protections against workplace discrimination even further. As a California Supreme Court justice, Janice Rogers Brown questioned whether a law prohibiting age discrimination really "inures to the benefit of public." Forget capability and the value of experience, the younger workforce will give more years to the corporation. In other cases, often as the sole dissenter from the rest of the California court, she wanted to limit the rights of disabled workers to seek relief from the courts.

Brown was confirmed, as part of the Senate compromise over the nuclear option, to the Court of Appeals for the D.C. Circuit. That court, considered the nation's second most powerful, hears more labor law cases than any other federal appeals court.

Another of Bush's extreme nominees, Terrence Boyle,

aggressively tried to limit discrimination claims as a U.S. district judge in North Carolina. Boyle attempted, essentially, to invalidate the Americans with Disabilities Act by making the burden of proof on disabled persons impossibly high. Unbelievably, he wrote in one case that the actual language of the act "has no force of law and is not binding on any court." If laws passed by Congress and signed by the president do not have "force of law," then which laws do? And what is judicial activism if not this?

Appeals courts overruled Boyle's decisions in 25 percent of the employment cases he tried. In June 2005, the Senate Judiciary Committee forwarded his nomination to the full Senate. To stop him, Democrats will be forced to resort to a filibuster.

The bottom line: it may be your dream job, you may have spent years training for it, you may be perfectly qualified, but if your boss doesn't like gays or thinks you're too old—well, sorry. Find another job. You see, it isn't your choice, it's theirs—and they can be as unfair as they want to be.

REPRODUCTION

In 1970 Norma McCorvey, a twenty-one-year-old Texan who had dropped out of ninth grade and was in her third pregnancy, became the lead plaintiff in a class-action suit against Texas's strict laws against abortion. The question in the case: whether she and others like her had the legal right to an abortion even if their lives were not in danger.

In 1973, in the landmark decision of *Roe v. Wade* (McCorvey was "Jane Roe"), the Supreme Court ruled by a 7-2 majority that she did have the right. (McCorvey had by then given birth to a girl.) The Court's rationale: that the constitutional right to privacy, by then entrenched in legal precedent, was "broad enough to encompass a woman's decision whether or not to terminate her pregnancy."

In the thirty years since, debate over reproductive rights has focused on whether *Roe* should be overturned. Religious zealots leave no doubt about their view, which some of them have expressed through bombings and murder.

They have succeeded in whittling away at *Roe*'s protections bit by bit. In a 1992 case, the Supreme Court upheld *Roe* but also approved of a variety of restrictions (waiting periods, anti-abortion counseling) that various states have imposed.

In 2003, Congress passed the Partial-Birth Abortion Ban Act of 2003. President Bush signed it in front of a group of smiling legislators—all men. The language of the act is so broad that it might cover even first-trimester abortions. So far, a number of federal appeals courts have ruled the ban unconstitutional. The reason: it does not contain, as Supreme Court precedent requires, an exception for cases where the health of the woman is in danger. Courts have invalidated on that basis a number of laws limiting abortion—ultraconservatives just seem to have a hard time remembering it!

Notice that they are not pressing legislation that includes those few additional words. Such a law would withstand judicial scrutiny, but it would also take the issue (to some degree) off the table. I'm not sure the Far Right wants to do that just yet.

No limits on abortion rights will ever be enough for the extremist religious conservatives—abortion rights must be abolished altogether. Yet Scalia has complained that "the mansion of constitutionalized abortion law, constructed overnight in *Roe v. Wade*, must be disassembled doorjamb by doorjamb, and never entirely brought down, no matter how wrong it may be." Actually, if you ask a lot of conservative political consultants, this subject is too big a rallying cry for them to really want it gone altogether.

In the meantime, Bush's extreme-right judicial nominees to the appellate courts will continue to chip away at *Roe*. As previously mentioned, William Pryor, who has been confirmed as a judge to the Eleventh Circuit, has called the decision the "worst abomination of constitutional law in our history."

Another nominee, Priscilla Owen, did her utmost as a Texas judge to limit the abortion rights of minors. Supreme Court precedent allows states to pass laws that require parental consent before a minor gets an abortion. However, the case law recognizes that in certain circumstances this will be impossible. Minors must therefore have the right to obtain what is called a "judicial bypass" —a court order, under limited circumstances, will allow them to go ahead with an abortion.

In nearly every case that she heard as a Texas judge, Owen refused such a judicial bypass when requested by a minor. She also tried to rewrite the Texas statute to make the bypass even harder to get. Her colleague on the Texas Supreme Court, Alberto Gonzales (a staunch conservative himself, he is now the U.S. attorney general) called her decision in one of these cases an "unconscionable act of judicial activism." Owen is now a judge on the Court of Appeals for the Fifth Circuit.

Because the Supreme Court will never review all of their

decisions, appellate judges like Pryor and Owen may well be able to limit the practical application of *Roe* in their jurisdictions. But what about *Roe* itself? It is not as safe as you might think. If President Bush is able to appoint a replacement for just one of the Court's moderate justices, then there might well be enough votes on the Court to overturn *Roe*.

That, of course, would be disastrous, but the extremist religious agenda would not stop there. Joseph Scheidler of the Pro-Life Action League has said that he "would like to outlaw contraception...contraception is disgusting—people using each other for pleasure." Impossible? The right of married couples to use contraception has only been protected a little longer than abortion rights. And recently, some pharmacists have been asserting the right not to fill prescriptions that they have a "moral" or "religious" objection to. And a number of these pharmacists are refusing to return the prescription to the patient—thus preventing them from going elsewhere without a return trip to their doctors.

In the meantime, President Bush has also stacked the Department of Health and Human Services with officials who say that condoms don't work to prevent sexually transmitted disease and that the best cure for PMS is prayer. These are the people who oversee federal programs promoting sexual health!

Congress and the president have spent hundreds of millions of taxpayer dollars on one of these programs—"abstinence-only" sex education. Public-health experts believe these programs deny young people the information they need to make intelligent decisions about sex. No scientific evidence proves that the programs work. (The programs do, however, provide a stealthy means to import the teaching of religion—one public-school program in Louisiana taught that abstention "will…[make you] really, truly 'cool' in God's eyes.")

When it comes to controlling your sexual and reproductive destiny, it isn't just that you can't decide what is best for you. You don't even deserve the information that would enable you to decide. It just isn't your choice.

DEATH

As maddening as the ultraconservatives are when it comes to reproductive rights, nothing is more upsetting, more unjust, more hateful than their position on end-of-life issues. Medical technology now allows us to prolong our lives well beyond what would have been possible even a few years ago. The framers could never have envisioned these advances in their wildest dreams.

But the additional time often comes at a steep price— agonizing pain, a loss of control of bodily functions, a slow slide into mental incapacity. Millions of us, unfortunately, are likely to undergo lingering deaths of this kind; many of us have already looked on in sorrow as a loved one suffered a similar fate.

In the extreme Right's world, if you have an incurable condition and are in great pain, you may not end your suffering. No matter how much pain you endure, no matter if you will never get better—if your life can be preserved, it *must* be.

Can the cruelty of this be exaggerated? When it comes to abortion, right-to-life activists claim that they speak for unborn children who don't have a voice of their own. But who do they speak for when it comes to end-of-life issues? Obviously *not* the patient who might choose to die—religious conservatives in effect tell the patient to shut up and keep suffering. (One of their arguments against birth control, remember, is that it allows women to avoid the God-ordained pain of childbirth!)

Most Americans flatly disagree with them. Seventy percent of us now favor laws allowing physician-assisted suicide. Sixty-four percent believe that doctor-assisted suicide should be a right recognized by the Supreme Court.

But the law and the courts have been slow to catch up. Thirty-eight states currently ban assisted suicide. Many of these laws were passed with the help of right-wing fear mongering. One of their favorite arguments is that doctors will start killing off poor people who can't pay the cost of keeping themselves alive.

The Supreme Court has upheld state laws banning assisted suicide. In a 1997 case involving a ban by Washington State, Justice Rehnquist wrote that "assistance in committing suicide is not a fundamental liberty interest" protected by the Constitution. The Court deferred to the judgment of Washington legislators and left the law in place. All nine justices concurred in the judgment.

The ruling did not prohibit states from *allowing* assisted suicide, however; it merely said that there was no fundamental right to it. In 1994 Oregon voters approved the Death With Dignity Act. The law includes a series of provisions to protect the vulnerable (again, ultraconservatives love to argue that, despite the Hippocratic Oath, doctors would start pulling the plug willy-nilly on indigent patients or better yet, conspire with inheritance-hungry relatives.) It requires that at least two doctors agree that the patient has fewer than six months to live. The patient must request assistance with suicide at least three times, and there is a fifteen-day waiting period. An avalanche of deaths has yet to occur. Only 170 Oregonians in eleven years have used the law, under which doctors prescribe a lethal dose of medicine that is administered by the patients themselves.

In November 2001, President Bush's attorney general John Ashcroft—once a champion of states' rights—issued the "Ashcroft Directive." The directive attempted to gut Oregon's law, threatening doctors who assisted patients under the Death With Dignity Act with prosecution under a federal law designed to limit drug trafficking.

The Ninth Circuit said the "attorney general's unilateral attempt to regulate general medical practices historically entrusted to state lawmakers...far exceeds the scope of his authority." The Supreme Court will hear the case in October 2005. The Court seems unlikely to recognize assisted suicide as a fundamental right. It may or may not defer to the judgment of Oregon voters. One hopes, however, that it will stop ultraconservatives like Ashcroft from twisting federal law to follow their lead.

Extremist religious conservatives are free to use every means available to prolong their own lives if they believe that is God's will. But they should not—and courts should not allow them to—compel others to undergo the same torment.

You have a terminal disease and are in constant, acute pain. There is no hope for a cure. You would prefer to die with dignity.

It is not your choice.

Extremist conservatives' attempts to prolong the lives of the terminally ill contrast starkly with their zeal to execute criminals. The most extreme fringes, particularly, favor expanding the use of the death penalty aggressively.

Why? Because the Bible says so, of course. In fact, the Bible prescribes death as the penalty for a lot of offenses—including blasphemy, homosexuality, idolatry, prostitution, Sabbath-breaking, and of course, adultery. (More than a few members of the Congress and clergy had better look out.) Extremist evangelicals who advocate a return to "biblical law" advocate a return to *this*.

This eagerness to kill criminals is very disturbing. In the ten years between 1992 and 2002, nearly fifty people were released from death row after it was discovered they were actually innocent. The errors in the process didn't occur in just one place—more than twenty states have had to release inmmates found to be innocent. In 2000, Illinois's governor imposed a moratorium on the death penalty because more people had been exonerated in that state (thirteen) than executed (twelve).

Despite the potential for error, ultraconservatives believe that a sentence of death should be carried out quickly. They would limit the constitutional protections afforded to convicts. Unfortunately, the Supreme Court has at times cooperated in expediting capital punishment.

Robert Alton Harris was due to die in California's gas chamber at San Quentin on April 21, 1992. A few days earlier, on Friday, April 17, death-row inmates filed a class action arguing that the gas chamber was a cruel and unusual punishment and therefore unconstitutional. Over the next four days various courts issued a

The Supreme Court vacated orders of the lower court that would have delayed Harris's execution so the gas chamber issue could be litigated. When the lower court tried to find other grounds for delay, the Court tersely refused: "No further stays of Robert Alton Harris's execution shall be entered by the federal courts except upon order of this Court." You may not care about the gas chamber debate, but I was bothered when the Court did not explain what gave it the authority to prohibit *all* future claims in the case (what if admissible evidence of Harris's innocence had emerged?).

Interestingly, the extreme Right points to increased DNA testing as proof the system can and will catch all cases of wrongful conviction through the miracle of science. Too bad the vast majority of criminal cases (including capital offenses) have no DNA evidence to test. So much for that argument.

The Court is currently closely divided on capital punishment. In 2005 it voted 5-4 to outlaw the execution of minors. Justice O'Connor voted against the majority in the case, so the confirmation of John Roberts would not change the outcome. But the appointment of one additional justice by the current administration could.

Extremist evangelicals hated the decision, of course. What do you mean we can't kill kids? They called for the impeachment of Justice Kennedy, who noted that other countries find the practice of juvenile execution abhorrent, and the impeachment of any congressmen who wouldn't vote to impeach him. James Dobson called Kennedy "the most dangerous man in America."

The extreme religious Right claims to zealously protect the lives of the innocent. But as we have seen, it won't even allow you to take your own life in the face of intolerable, and incurable, pain. How then can it support a system of capital punishment that has undoubtedly executed innocent people, and will almost certainly continue to do so?

The answer is the same one that Justice Scalia gave to justify the Texas anti-sodomy law—because it's "moral."

But the real point, as always, is this: *they* define what is moral. You don't. For them it is *never* going to be your choice.

The judges nominated by President Bush in the next three years could and most likely *will* profoundly alter the makeup of the federal appellate courts in the many areas already discussed. One thing is certain: the extreme Right will not give up its mission to completely capture our courts—or back off its assault on our fundamental freedoms.

In the words of a training manual written for the Free Congress Foundation, an ultraconservative think tank closely connected to the Bush administration, "Our movement will be entirely destructive...We will not try to reform the existing institutions. We only intend to weaken them, and eventually destroy them."

POT AND KETTLE

Will the Real Judicial Tyrants Please Stand Up?

The problem with all the extreme Right's whining about "judicial activism" is that conservative judges engage in it at least as often as their liberal counterparts. Consider the following analysis reported in the *New York Times* on July 6, 2005. The *Times* looked at Supreme Court cases since 1994 where justices "substituted" their opinions for those of the Republican-dominated Congress. The following list shows the percentage of these cases in which a justice voted to *strike down* a federal law as constitutional:

Thomas	65.63%
Kennedy	64.06%
Scalia	56.25%
Rehnquist	46.88%
O'Connor	46.77%
Souter	42.19%
Stevens	39.34%
Ginsburg	39.06%
Breyer	28.13%

The extreme Right loves to demand that judges who don't "know their place" should be impeached. After reading the *Times* article, should Thomas and Scalia be worried?

POT AND PAIN

The Court and the Commerce Clause

Not only does the extreme Right want to prolong your pain, they want to deny you ways to treat it. James Dobson's Focus on the Family calls efforts to legalize medical marijuana "incrementalism"—the first step in a bid to put all illegal drugs on the counter at your local drugstore.

The Supreme Court has cooperated in attempts to limit the use of marijuana for medical use. Two California women, one with an inoperable brain tumor and the other with a degenerative spine disease, had tried all sorts of medications to ease their pain. When everything else failed, they began growing pot in their backyard. California law allowed them to smoke marijuana to ease their pain.

Federal law, however, did not, and the Bush administration tried to prosecute the two women. The Court agreed that it could, finding that the federal government has the right to prohibit marijuana use by anyone as part of Congress's power to regulate "interstate commerce." The Court said that exempting backyard pot from federal regulation would have a "substantial impact" on the interstate market for marijuana.

The ruling was a flat retreat from other recent decisions in which the Court limited Congress's power to pass laws under the Constitution's Commerce Clause. Remember that the Court struck down federal laws prohibiting guns near school zones and protecting women against domestic abuse.

More than one commentator said that the Court is willing to allow states to do what they want—except when it comes to California!

If you want to alleviate your pain, once again it simply isn't your choice.

CHAPTER EIGHTEEN
PUBLIC BIBLE SCHOOL

Bushwick High School's gnarled iron gates have seen thousands of students come and go. *The Honeymooners'* Jackie Gleason attended Bushwick. The nondescript school building in Brooklyn, New York, has stood witness to the declining fortunes of the surrounding neighborhood. It has weathered delinquency, street crime, teacher's strikes, and shrinking school budgets. But now Bushwick High has surrendered to a weekly invasion.

Each weekend the school is converted, literally. Every Sunday morning a small army unloads the trucks that line up along Irving Avenue, carrying tables, chairs, food, flowers, audio-visual equipment, translation headsets, cribs, banners, and musical instruments through the gates and inside the school.

Sundays at Bushwick High belong to the Christ Tabernacle Church. Like an occupation force, the eight-hundred-person-strong congregation transforms this public high school into an autonomous religious community. The school auditorium becomes a church, reverberating with upbeat modern gospel music. Classrooms that during the week teach the three Rs bear signs welcoming "Christ's Crusaders, Second and Third Grade."

Christ Tabernacle Church's pastor, Adam Durso, the general

leading this army's weekly invasion, is resolute. "We're here for the long haul," he says. And all over America religious zealots like Durso are crossing school thresholds with their flocks. In community after community, radical Christians are setting up shop. Not just on Sunday, but on every day of the week.

School officials seeking to keep private religion and public education separate are helpless in the face of a systematic, organized assault from fundamentalists. Financed by the same ultraconservative groups seeking to redraw the Bill Of Rights at every turn, evangelist missionaries have used the courts to force their way into schools all over the nation.

BLUE STATE BLUES

New York City is not pleased about Bushwick's weekly transformation into a Bible colony. To city and school-board officials, Christ Tabernacle's occupation of school property is a flagrant violation of the separation of church and state. "The diversity of this city is one of its greatest strengths," New York City government lawyer Lisa Grument points out. "We are concerned about having the neighborhood school—the public school—identified with a particular religious congregation."

For almost seventy-five years, New York has adamantly banned church services from public school buildings. Yet according to the *New York Times*, as of February 2005, "Two dozen churches and other religious groups...have found homes in New York City schools." There's no way the New York City school system would change that policy. Unless the courts forced them to.

And they did.

In 1997 an evangelical church called the Bronx Household of Faith unsuccessfully challenged New York school policy in a lawsuit against the city. In a unanimous decision, the three presiding judges hearing the case in the Second Circuit Court of Appeals found in favor of the school system. The panel concluded that it was perfectly reasonable for elected state and school-board officials to prohibit churches from using public school buildings for religious worship services. The judges unanimously upheld the Constitution's first clause of the First Amendment, separating church and state.

Federal and state judicial codes are crystal clear about appellants (parties bringing suit) repeating the same lawsuit over and over. There's barely room on court calendars for first-time hearings, let alone repeats. The law *does* permit a second chance if there has been an intervening change in the law. Or, if a higher court has made a ruling that has changed the legal playing field, the suit can be heard again.

Four years after their original day in court, the Bronx Household of Faith was back. Supported by the Beckett Fund for Religious Liberty (boasting both Orrin Hatch and Henry Hyde on its advisory board), the Household of Faith returned to the Second Circuit Court of Appeals. The U.S. Supreme Court's June 2001 *Good News Club v. Milford Central School District* decision was the key the Household of Faith used to get back. And it would become the key that opened the doors of public schools all over America to Christian evangelists.

The Household of Faith's "meetings" included prayer, testimony from the faithful, "preaching the word of God," communion, and solicitation of donations. But its lawyers argued that the group's proposed use of the public schools was just for instruction from a "religious point of view." Pressed about the use of rituals like communion and baptism, church attorneys argued that these were no different than the Boy Scouts' flag salute.

For two of the three judges hearing the case, the Supreme Court's new 2001 ruling suggested a different outcome than before. This time, the house of faith won. The majority decision of the Second Circuit stated, in part, "We find no principled basis upon which to distinguish the activities set out by the Supreme Court in *Good News Club* from the activities that the Bronx Household of Faith has proposed for its Sunday meetings at Middle School 206B." In his minority decision, Judge Roger Miner (who had written the majority opinion in the 1997 case) stated, "Today, the Majority permits a public school building in the Bronx to be designated 'Middle School 206B and The Bronx Household of Faith.'"

Household of Faith won solely because of the Supreme Court's new *Good News Club* decision. *Good News* was the first falling domino in a radical Right avalanche that shows no sign of slowing.

GOOD NEWS BAD NEWS

With more than 4500 chapters in the U.S. and over 500 in 142 countries abroad, the Good News Club hosts after-school revival meetings disguised as Bible study. Good News openly recruits children to become born-again Christians. The kids are led in songs with lyrics like "Good news: Jesus died for me; good news: I can be saved eternally," instructed in fundamentalist Christian dogma, and even encouraged to proselytize to any adult sinners they might know. "Through a child," says the GNC's parent organization, the Child Evangelism Fellowship, "entrance is gained to the heart and home of unsaved parents."

CEF's stated mission is to "not only bring children into a right relationship with God, but to discipline them in His Word and establish them in Bible teaching churches." Unfortunately, that church has become your local public school. The CEF through the Good News Clubs is, in the words of the *Washington Post*, "using schools as their mailrooms and eight-year-olds as their couriers."

Good News sells their brand of salvation to children using language that children understand. "Just like a ticket to the movies," an after-school minister explains to her preteen disciples, "you also need a ticket to heaven." But who printed Good News and the CEF a ticket to recruit children into fundamentalist doctrine on public school property?

It was the U.S. Supreme Court.

In 1996 the Reverend Stephen Fournier of Milford, New York, approached his village's sole public school about hosting a Good News Club chapter. Recognizing the Good News Ministry for what it was, the local school system turned Fournier down flat. The Good News Club was "Sunday School on Tuesday," said the Milford School District's attorney, Frank W. Miller. But the reverend knew where to go for some ultraconservative legal muscle and ready cash. Fourneur immediately contacted the Rutherford Institute.

Funded in part by Adolph Coors, the Rutherford Institute

fought California's child welfare agencies in a misguided effort to make child abuse a matter of "family values" instead of a crime. It also attempted to block sexual education classes in California schools. Rutherford founder John Whitehead's legal credentials were impeccable in radical-right circles. Whitehead had served as cocounsel for Paula Corbin Jones in her dismissed lawsuit against President Bill Clinton.

Rutherford attorneys realized the best approach to demolishing the wall between church and state was to go around it. "The schools teach about Marxism; they're not endorsing that. They teach about the Holocaust; they're not endorsing that. They teach about the Klu Klux Klan; they're certainly not endorsing that," Reverend Fournier told reporters. His legal team intended to plead their case not as a matter of religious freedom but as an issue of free speech.

"Congress shall make no law respecting establishment of religion..." says the first clause in the Bill of Rights. This establishment clause is the foundation of separation of church and state. With the backing of the Rutherford Institute, Fournier and the Good News Club would simply smuggle their fundamentalist agenda into public schools. Leapfrogging over the establishment clause, they would undo 175 years of rulings that preserved the division between pulpit and government.

SUPREME SACRIFICE

With the Rutherford Institute on board, Fournier won a temporary injunction that allowed him to hold club meetings at the school. But the Northern District Court of New York ruled for the Milford School District, as did the Second Circuit U.S. Court of Appeals. So, armed with a state court decision from 1994 that permitted a Good News Club in Missouri to meet on school property, the Reverend Fournier's attorneys persuaded the U.S. Supreme Court to review their case.

On March 1, 2001, the Supreme Court heard testimony from both sides in the case. "If I say 'ha ha,' I'm allowed in the forum, but if I say 'amen,' I'm excluded," argued Thomas Marcelle, representing Good News. Marcelle also invoked a 1993 case in which a church group on Long Island was permitted to screen religious movies on a public school campus. But in that case the audience wasn't made up of children and the gathering was held in the evening, not immediately after school like Good News.

Justice David Souter latched on to the distinction. "In this case you don't have a sophisticated group of people of college age who know the university is not proselytizing them," he said. Milford School District's Frank Miller offered that headquartering the club in a school building immediately after the last bell had rung "might potentially be divisive." Justice Antonin Scalia would hear none of it. He laid into Miller's arguments every chance he got, finally dismissing Milford's position by saying, "I'm glad I don't live in New York anymore."

Unfortunately for the Constitution, Scalia's side prevailed. The Supreme Court ruled in favor of Good News Clubs. The establishment clause of the First Amendment was barely mentioned. The constitutional bedrock that legally separates church from state had been pushed aside. Justice Clarence Thomas's majority opinion stated in part, "We cannot say the danger that children would misperceive the endorsement of religion is any greater than the danger that they would perceive a hostility toward the religious viewpoint if the club were excluded from the public forum."

This "hostility" argument has been played to death but keeps on working. By not permitting religion in every place that general organizations are allowed, governments, schools, and other public groups are somehow oppressing religion. This argument would not pass Logic 101.

But Justice Souter wrote a withering dissent. In Souter's words, the Court's 6-3 decision put forth "the remarkable proposition that any public school opened for civic meetings must be opened for use as a church, synagogue, or mosque." Souter hadn't been taken in by the free speech smokescreen. Good News was "an evangelical service of worship calling children to commit themselves in an act of Christian conversion." The majority opinion "ignores reality."

"At least five justices see no distinction between talking about religion, worshipping, and recruiting young children to the faith," said Reverend Barry Lynn of Americans United for Separation of Church and State . Reverend Lynn predicted the decision would "create a battlefield out of America's elementary schools." And that's precisely what has happened.

As soon as the Court's judgment came down, right-wing legal groups like the Liberty Counsel and Pat Robertson's American Center for Law and Justice switched into high gear. Armed with a ticket the Court had printed, religious extremists combed the country in search of situations comparable to Reverend Fournier's.

Good News Clubs swooped into schools from coast to coast.
But in the spring of 2001, students at a Milwaukee, Wisconsin, elementary school told their principal, Dorothy Smith, that Good News Club's fire and brimstone sermons were scaring them. Acting, she thought, in the best interests of the school, Smith canceled the club meetings. Ms. Smith was promptly served with a letter from the Liberty Counsel implying impending legal action if the club wasn't immediately reinstated. "Our school district has shallow pockets and couldn't afford the fight," Smith told the *New York Times*. She had no choice but to permit the club to reconvene. Liberty's financial strong-arm tactics worked.

Then, in September of 2001, the Child Evangelism Fellowship began Good News Club services at two Connecticut elementary schools. Served notice by CEF, John F. Kennedy Elementary principal Warren Logee was forced to give the Good News Club a cordial welcome. "The group was knowledgeable about the laws and court cases dealing with the issue," Logee said , "and they made the assumption that this was something they were entitled to do." And in the lengthening shadow of the Supreme Court's ruling, it was.

State by state, public campuses have been forced to open their doors to born-again ministries that aggressively covet grade-school souls. The ACLJ successfully pushed through Good News Club meetings previously banned in Omaha, Texas; Boston, Massachusetts; and Vallejo, California, over the objections of their respective school boards. Montgomery County, Maryland, schools were forced to let Good News Club missionaries distribute flyers and tracts on school grounds. Backed by Christian fundamentalist lawyers, nineteen-year-old Tausha Prince was permitted to proselytize after school at her Seattle-area high school. And in St. Martin's Parish in New Orleans, high school senior Dominique Begnaud was given permission to do the same.

When the *New York Times* asked a Connecticut mother about her child's participation in a Good News chapter, her response was, "It beats being home in front of the TV." So in addition to salvation, the Good News Club's ministry offers parents an alternative to cartoons. There may be little wrong about using a fundamentalist religious organization as a babysitter. But there's something disturbing about a ministry willing to create a generation of spiritual latchkey kids. And there's something very, very wrong about a court that upholds the right of a few parochial zealots to have an unending pool of converts supplied by our country's public school systems.

STEEPLECHASE

When empaneled to hear the Bronx Household of Faith case a second time, Judge Roger Miner (the same federal judge who presided in the Baby Jane Doe case) listened in horror as his fellow judges cited the Supreme Court's *Good News Club* precedent and outvoted him 2-1. In his dissenting opinion, Miller made sure to single out a brief filed in favor of the Household of Faith by the Bush Justice Department. To Miner, the Bush lawyers were hypocrites, "especially given the current administration's policies favoring state and local control over education and its aversion to 'activist federal judges' who seek to substitute their judgment in the place of democratically elected state and local policymakers."

Judge Miner also unearthed a previous Clarence Thomas opinion in a Missouri desegregation case that illustrated the high court's evident double standard. "We have long recognized that education is primarily a concern of local authorities," Thomas wrote in a concurring opinion that left desegregation up to the schools. "Federal courts do not possess the capabilities of state and local school officials in addressing difficult educational problems. State and local school officials not only bear the responsibility for educational decisions, they also are better equipped than a single federal judge to make the day-to-day policy, curricular, and funding choices necessary to bring a school district into compliance with the Constitution." Apparently, Thomas will defer to the judgments of local school boards if they reject racial integration. But if a radical fundamentalist church group wishes to recruit in a public elementary school, Thomas will hold the door open.

CHAPTER NINETEEN
COURTING BIG BUSINESS

Extreme right-wingers love to claim that liberal "activist" judges interpret the Constitution however they see fit. Conservative judges, supposedly, do nothing of the sort. Instead, they "faithfully interpret" the Constitution as it was "originally intended."

Only this isn't true. In fact, ultraconservative judges like Scalia, Thomas, and Rehnquist do just the opposite. In order to advance their hard-line agenda, these justices come up with a decision they like and then fix the logic to support it. This isn't just judicial activism—it's rewriting history and precedent to *support* judicial activism. More importantly, these decisions almost always favor big corporations over the little guy. Not only are these judges hypocrites, they are hypocrites at the expense of the average American.

Two varied but important fields underscore both this duplicity and its detrimental effects on Americans—punitive damages and campaign finance reform. In cases involving both these issues, ultraconservative justices, supported with faulty logic from hard-line right-wing think tanks, have ruled for corporate America and against the average citizen. In both areas they have done so without regard for history or judicial precedent.

One day in 1981, Curtis and Inez Campbell were driving on a highway in their home state of Utah. Traffic was slow and Curtis was impatient, so he decided to try to pass six trucks ahead of him by driving on the wrong side of the road. Before Campbell could complete this risky and dangerous maneuver, he almost collided with another car traveling in the opposite direction, driven by a man named Todd Ospital. To avoid colliding with Campbell, Ospital swerved onto the shoulder and slammed into another car, driven by Robert Slusher. When the dust from this tragic multicar crash had settled, Ospital was dead and Slusher was permanently disabled. Campbell, miraculously, walked away unscathed.

State Farm was Curtis Campbell's auto insurance carrier. For years Campbell had been a loyal customer, and now State Farm was obligated to fulfill its end of the bargain. Both the police and State Farm's investigators had concluded that Campbell was a hundred percent at fault for the accident. Furthermore, as stated in Campbell's insurance plan, State Farm's maximum financial responsibility in the lawsuits was $50,000—$25,000 each for Ospital and Slusher. The decent and legal thing for State Farm to do would have been to pay out the policy limit of $50,000, leaving Campbell to deal with the situation he had created. (Both families could have then sued Campbell on top of the insurance settlement, which State Farm had no obligation to assist.) State Farm's actions were a no-brainer given the stipulations of Campbell's policy and his clear fault in the accident.

But State Farm didn't do the decent thing. It didn't think it had to—with a net worth of over $43 billion, it decided to dispute the claim. It argued that Campbell was not responsible for the death and injuries. It also assured the Campbells that they were not legally responsible for the accident and that State Farm's strategy was in their best interest. This was a very risky maneuver. If State Farm lost the trial, they would be required to pay whatever damages the jury awarded, regardless of the $50,000 policy limit.

This strategy wasn't used out of benevolence for the Campbells. Unbeknownst to the Campbells, it was based on State Farm's "Performance, Planning, and Review" policy. The goal of the policy, adopted by State Farm's senior management, was to use "the claims-adjustment process as a profit center." Specifically, the policy was designed to pay out less than fair amounts to clients in order to enhance the company's bottom line. In other words: State Farm's *stated company policy* was to reduce or not make payment to claimants in order to make more money.

This is big business at its worst, and things only got uglier. According to the plan, State Farm's first course of action in disputing a claim was to attack the character of the victim, making false notations in his claim file. In the Campbells' case, the State Farm claim agent changed the accident report to state that Ospital had been speeding to visit his pregnant girlfriend at the time of the accident. Not only had Ospital not been speeding, but he didn't even have a girlfriend! State Farm lied about the victim of a crippling accident so it wouldn't have to pay him.

It didn't take long for the Campbells to realize their faith in State Farm had been misplaced. The jury came back with a verdict for the victims, finding that Curtis Campbell had been completely at fault for the accident, and awarded the victims

$185,849 in damages—nearly four times the amount that State Farm could have settled the case for without going to trial. Then State Farm, in keeping with its unethical and blatantly illegal tactics, outright refused to pay the difference. Having previously assured the Campbells of their financial safety, the multibillion-dollar corporation saddled them with the $135,849 bill. The person in charge of their claim told them to put "for sale signs on [their] property to get things moving. "

The Campbells then teamed up with their accident victims and sued State Farm, arguing that the company had acted unreasonably in refusing to initially settle the victims' claims for $50,000. They won the case—the jury awarded the Campbells $2.6 million in damages to compensate them for their losses, as well as an additional $145 million in punitive damages.

That sounds like a lot of money, and it is. Punitive damages like this, though, aren't awarded every day; they are delivered *only* in cases in which a defendant has acted "recklessly and intentionally." They are awarded in large sums so huge multinational corporations like State Farm are deterred from acting criminally again. Even though the $145 million figure was high, the Utah Supreme Court upheld the award on appeal. The Utah Supreme Court—not exactly a bastion of judicial liberals— sided with the little guy. State Farm, it knew, was rich enough to shrug off $2.6 million. But it would have a hard time shrugging off $145 million. The company needed to be taught a lesson, and the whopping punitive damages sum would do exactly that.

State Farm decided to appeal the case to the U.S. Supreme Court, and that's where the radical Right flexed its muscle.

Amicus curiae, or "friend of the court," briefs poured in from ultraconservative think tanks like Citizens for a Sound Economy, insisting the decision be struck down. Their reasoning was that punitive damages had gotten too high and the Court had to stop this. This was the *exact activist logic* hard-liners accuse liberals of advocating. The support for overturning the Campbell decision came from a cadre of far-right intellectuals intent on legislating from the bench.

That the Court decided to hear the case out of the thousands presented before it was rather activist to begin with. Not only that, the Court then decided in favor of State Farm, ruling the size of the punitive damages unconstitutional. In making this conclusion, it also divined a formula for the appropriate measure for punitive damages: ten to one. The Court said that punitive damages were unconstitutional if they were more than ten times the amount of compensation damages. That's not all—the Rehnquist Court also ruled that when the compensation damages were large in the first place, any greater punitive award was unconstitutional. The Court, on recommendations from numerous conservative think tanks, reversed the Utah Supreme Court's earlier decision to punish State Farm. As the punitive damages awarded to the Campbells far exceeded the Rehnquist Court's arbitrary amount, the Court ordered that most of the award be cut.

Whatever happened to the right wing's heralded position that policy issues be left to state courts rather than decided by unelected federal judges? And what about Scalia, Thomas, and Rehnquist's prior insistence that constitutional rules be grounded in the text of the Constitution and what its framers intended? These stances don't seem to matter when big business is the defendant. In a blatant display of hypocrisy, this contingent went against its stated ideological position in order to save a corporation from justifiable punishment. Not only did hard-line conservative justices change their tune, but so did numerous policy institutes devoted to this very issue.

Regardless of your position on punitive damage (I have been critical of many aspects of the same), there is *no* provision in the Constitution limiting punitive damages, much less any reference to a particular ratio for calculating these awards. These same ultraconservative justices—Rehnquist, Thomas, and Scalia—declared the use of the trimester system in *Roe v. Wade* a completely arbitrary system of determining constitutionality. Given all of these inconsistencies, how could the Rehnquist Court justify giving big business a break when it came to punitive damages?

It couldn't, but that doesn't mean it didn't try. The primary justification offered by the justices was that punitive damages awards had gotten out of control, implying that state courts and legislatures hadn't tried to limit them. Too bad none of this was true.

State legislatures were working to limit punitive damages all across America as the Campbell case moved through the justice system. During this time, seventeen state legislatures passed laws making it harder for juries to award punitive damages. They could handle the issue on their own. Eight states also passed laws mandating that the amount of punitive damages awarded by juries be limited by the amount of compensatory damages awarded. In Colorado, punitive damages awarded could no longer exceed compensatory damages awarded; in Florida, most punitive damages awards could not exceed three times the amount of the compensatory damages awarded; in Kansas...you get the idea. Other states were restricting punitive damages by forcing them to be pooled toward state resources rather than paid to defendants. Other states capped awards entirely, usually below the $1 million mark.

In other words, state legislatures were doing exactly what the Rehnquist Court reasoned they weren't doing. Laws were being passed, legislatures were acting—all in accordance with a conservative political philosophy. But that wasn't enough. So when a big corporation came before the high court with a very specific request, the hard-line conservatives knew what they had to do, even if it meant contradicting their own publicly stated judicial philosophies. It was naked judicial activism at its worst, aimed at hurting the little guy, not punishing the corporate villain, and then abetting State Farm without regard for the devastating consequences of its actions.

To appreciate the size of the victory that the Rehnquist Court handed to big business, and the corresponding defeat it dealt to average Americans, consider some of the cases decided in the wake of the Campbells' case. In *Philip Morris USA Inc. v. Williams*, the Supreme Court set aside a $79.5 million punitive damages award that had been upheld on appeal by the Oregon courts. In this case, the jury had found that a widow's husband—who had been a smoker—had died of lung cancer due to the fraudulent behavior of Philip Morris. In particular, the jury had found that Philip Morris had not only failed to investigate the safety of its tobacco products, but that it knew its products were unsafe and marketed them anyway. This had been part of Philip Morris's business strategy for more than forty years! Not that this mattered to the Rehnquist Court. Like the Campbell decision, and despite clear evidence of the intentional wrongdoing of big business, the Court knocked down the punitive damages.

In another case, *Ford Motor Co. v. Estate of Smith*, the Supreme Court set aside a Kentucky court award of $15 million in punitive damages. In this case, the victim was killed after a Ford pickup truck crushed him against a storage shed after the vehicle shifted from park to reverse due to defective design. The trial revealed that Ford knew of this problem for over seven years prior to Smith's death, yet still continued to make trucks with the defect. Given this obvious evidence of wrongdoing on Ford's part, and even though the Kentucky courts reduced the jury's punitive damages award from $20 million to $15 million on appeal, the Supreme Court still drastically reduced the punitive damages.

There are many more cases like these. They repeatedly demonstrate that hard-line conservatives put large corporate interests above the interests of average citizens and will even use the courts, despite asserting contrary judicial ideology. On the other hand, even when scores of people die and lower courts rule that a corporation's actions put "tens of thousands of lives at risk" (as one did in yet another case the Rehnquist Court overturned), the right-wing Supreme Court and hard-line conservatives side with the big boys. Intellectual honesty demands that this issue be handled in our legislatures—not the courts.

Punitive damages are not the only area in which the reactionary right wing demonstrates blatant hypocrisy—campaign finance is another. This is also because of the ultra-Right's allegiance to big business. Since the ultra-Right couldn't prevent campaign finance laws from being passed in Congress—laws like the McCain-Feingold Act, which eliminated "soft" money in politics—the reactionary Right turned to the courts, hoping this branch of government would do its bidding. For decades, big business interests like the tobacco, health care, insurance, and automobile industries have used soft-money donations to buy off legislators on both sides. Reforming the system meant that the reactionary Right would have to give up some of its political influence, and so it moved to overturn actions finally passed by Congress and signed by the president.

Having failed to prevent the McCain-Feingold Act from being passed, the right wing turned to its allies on the federal bench for help and filed a lawsuit to have the law declared unconstitutional. Specifically, they argued that campaign contributions by corporations were a form of political speech protected by the First Amendment. Once again, the court was pressed asked the courts to engage in judicial activism by declaring a federal law unconstitutional. The reactionary Right (again) demanded that the courts interpret the Constitution to find for their side, against their professed belief that the Constitution's text be strictly construed. This is the highest order of hypocrisy.

Fortunately, this attempt largely failed when a 5-4 decision upheld most of the act's provisions in 2003. But Justices Scalia and

Thomas—the two favored justices of the reactionary Right—wrote scathing dissents, arguing that the act violated the First Amendment. According to Justice Scalia, the day the Court announced its decision upholding the act was "a sad day for the freedom of speech." Justice Thomas agreed, writing: "The Court today upholds what can only be described as the most significant abridgment of the freedoms of speech and association since the Civil War."

In order to justify their opinions, Scalia and Thomas equate money with free speech. Of course, saying that huge political contributions are the same as speech means rich Americans are heard much more loudly throughout our government. More importantly, no such justification exists in the Constitution. Both the text itself and the words and deeds of the framers unequivocally demonstrate that campaigning is not tantamount to political speech.

The framers went even further than this—they believed any campaigning at all was wrong, an evil to our political process that should be avoided at all costs. The reason the framers drafted the Constitution in the first place was not to ensure but to limit the power of a particular minority over the majority. The framers wanted elected officials to act in the best interests of the nation as a whole, not in the interest of a powerful few.

One of the ways that the framers tried to accomplish this objective was by requiring that each congressional district contain at least 30,000 people. In 1789, without campaigning tools like television and radio, this would insure that each district was simply too large for a candidate to reach everyone. Door-to-door canvassing and glad-handing simply couldn't dent the sheer size of the district. In essence, the framers didn't want candidates to campaign for office.

The express size of congressional districts would make such campaigning virtually impossible—intentionally. James Wilson, the delegate who proposed the 30,000-person congressional district limit, said, "There is no danger of improper elections if made by large districts. Bad elections proceed from smallness of the districts which give an opportunity to bad men to intrigue themselves into office." The only time during the entire Constitutional Convention when George Washington spoke was to defend this provision.

Any doubt about the framers' distaste for campaigning was dispelled when James Madison introduced the Bill of Rights on the floor of the newly elected House of Representatives. Most people don't realize that the original Bill of Rights included twelve amendments, only ten of which were eventually adopted. The very first one of those twelve amendments increased the minimum size of a congressional district from 30,000 to 50,000 people. Although this failed, the fact that it was the first amendment proposed undoubtedly demonstrates the founders' clear intent to severely limit the possibility for politicians to campaign.

The hypocrisy of the reactionary Right contradicts even the words and deeds of the founding fathers themselves. Justices Scalia, Thomas, and Rehnquist ignore not only the framers' intent but also their stated beliefs. The text of the Constitution, and the intention of the framers, could not have been more clearly against campaigning, and the detriments of the influence of special-interest groups at the expense of the nation. In his celebrated farewell address, George Washington warned against the "constant danger of excess" among special-interest groups. For Scalia and Thomas to claim that restrictions on campaigning contradict the First Amendment is both ridiculous and intellectually dishonest. Indeed, the framers would no doubt have favored a law like McCain-Feingold because of its inherent skepticism of special interests in government.

As far as the right wing is concerned, the interests of big business trump the text of the Constitution as well as the intent of the framers themselves. Rather than decide based on history and judicial precedent, the ultraconservative justices on the Supreme Court have time and again done exactly the opposite. With the support of numerous ultra-right-wing organizations, Justices Scalia, Thomas, and Rehnquist have repeatedly fit the logic of decisions to outcomes they wanted. This is not just judicial activism—it's barefaced hypocrisy. And it's hypocrisy designed to protect the interests of a wealthy few over a majority of average Americans.

Say one thing, do another; it's a classic tactic by the radical Right. And worst of all, it's working.

CHAPTER TWENTY
THE LEGEND OF PAT GARRETT

Shortly before Labor Day in 1994, Patricia Garrett was diagnosed with breast cancer. For the next year she persevered through the removal of her breast, radiation treatments, and chemotherapy. She survived, thanks in no small part to her training as a nurse. But just when the nightmare of her ordeal with cancer was over, she had to live through another. The University of Alabama Hospital, where Garrett had worked for almost twenty years, decided that it didn't want a potentially sick nurse working there. She was fired.

While undergoing treatment for cancer, Garrett's supervisor first encouraged and later pressured her to take a leave of absence or transfer to a less prestigious job. She was told her supervisor didn't like "sick people," had earned a reputation for getting rid of them. In spite of this harassment, Garrett made it clear to him that she wished to continue working in her current job as the hospital's director of OB/GYN/Neonatal Services. In fact, even though Garrett continued with her chemotherapy and radiation, she excelled at her job. Rather than supporting and encouraging Garrett's courageous struggle, however, her supervisor continued threatening to transfer her to a less prestigious position. Eventually,

Garrett's supervisor asked one of her subordinates to do her job and ordered that Garrett be transferred to a temporary position at a satellite hospital.

In March 1995, Garrett complained to her doctor about the indignities to which she was being subjected at the hospital. Her doctor empathized and told her that this kind of workplace harassment provoked stress. Her doctor recommended that Garrett take a leave of absence for the duration of her treatment—a leave to which she was entitled according to the hospital's employee handbook. When Garrett returned to work four months later, her supervisor told her the hospital did not want her back. Her only options were to quit, accept a demotion, or be fired. Realizing she had no future at the hospital, Garrett began looking for a new job, but requested that she be allowed to stay on for a few more weeks so she could continue to be covered under the hospital's health insurance policy. This coverage was crucial to her ability to pay for her ongoing cancer treatments. The hospital denied her request. Left with no other options, Garrett left her job at the hospital and eventually found another job as a nurse manager at a convalescence home, where she had to take a $13,000 pay cut.

Garrett sued the University of Alabama Hospital in federal court for violating the Americans With Disabilities Act (ADA). The ADA, which Congress had passed in 1990 to prevent employers from discriminating against employees with physical and mental disabilities, protects more than forty-three million Americans from discrimination. Unfortunately, federal courts never got a chance to rule as to whether the hospital had violated the ADA. The reason stemmed from a series of 5-4 decisions beginning in the mid-

1990s, in which the Rehnquist Court struck down federal powers so much that states no longer had to compensate victims of illegal discrimination, even if Congress passed laws requiring them to do so.

Even though Garrett wasn't employed by the state but by a for-profit hospital, the Court ruled she still couldn't sue. In the name of states' rights, the Supreme Court ruled that thousands of state agencies—such as hospitals, university presses, and utilities—do not have to compensate discriminated persons under the ADA.

The doctrine of states' rights under which the Court ruled against Garrett has far-reaching implications. Historically, when ultra-right judges have interpreted the doctrine, the consequences have been disastrous. Using it, right-wing majorities in state legislatures were able to deny civil rights to African-Americans, women, the elderly, the disabled, and other minorities who didn't have the political power to stand up for themselves. Because of this inequality, Congress eventually passed federal laws protecting these groups from the misguided actions of the majority in state legislatures. But now, the ultra-Right and its allies on the Rehnquist Court are trying to take away federal protections by striking them down as unconstitutional. In doing so, the Rehnquist Court is saying that the same federal laws that require private institutions to treat everyone equally do not apply to the states or the thousands of agencies run by the states. This means that state governments—historically not the most progressive institutions—are now protected against discrimination lawsuits.

When the framers of the Constitution gathered in Philadelphia during the summer of 1787, one of their principal goals was to create a new system of government where powers were shared between a strong federal government and the individual state governments that already existed. Before the Revolutionary War, the power of government resided solely with the king of England. After American Independence, sovereignty resided in the thirteen individual state governments. With the adoption of the new Constitution in 1787, the framers embarked upon a radical new experiment that had never before been tried. They placed the sovereignty of both the state and federal governments in "the people." Hence the first words of the Constitution read: "We the people in order to form a more perfect union...do ordain and establish this Constitution."

The word "sovereign" never appears in the text of the Constitution. And nowhere does the Constitution say that states are sovereigns and don't have to compensate people whose rights they violate. Indeed, for-profit state agencies didn't even exist when the Constitution was drafted. Nevertheless, the extreme Right continues to extend this immunity to organizations like state university hospitals, even in the absence of any textual or historical basis for doing so.

For more than a century prior to the 1990s, the Supreme Court had ruled that both states and state agencies could be sued for damages in federal court for violations of federal law. All Congress had to do was be specific in drafting legislation, which it did in the case of the ADA. For this reason, when Congress passed the ADA in 1990, it provided that states—and state agencies like the University of Alabama Hospital—could be sued for damages in federal court if they discriminated against people like Patricia Garrett. Ms. Garrett and her attorneys expected this remedy when

they sued the University of Alabama Hospital. Neither Congress
nor Garrett and her attorneys could have prepared for the judicial
activism of the Rehnquist Court.

JUDICIAL ACTIVISM RUN AMOK

In the last ten years, in a series of 5-4 decisions, the far-right
justices on the Rehnquist Court have defended states' rights above
all else (except, of course, when they don't—eminent domain,
Kelo v. New London, medical marijuana, and other moments of
philosophical expedience). Specifically, they have allowed the fifty
state governments and thousands of for-profit state agencies to
violate federal laws passed to protect the rights of individuals like
you and me. In doing so, they have struck down the very federal
laws that permit suits to be brought against the states. And, to
accomplish their objective of resurrecting states' rights, they have
gone against all their sacred beliefs concerning the interpretation of
the Constitution. They have engaged in judicial activism to remove
the protections of ordinary Americans like Patricia Garrett.

In 1997, the Rehnquist Court ruled that Congress could not
write laws that permitted states to be sued when they violated
federal statutes. In essence, the Court created new standards that
Congress must meet before it could hold states accountable for
violating people's rights. One new provision was a requirement that
Congress be presented with clearly documented evidence showing
a history of "widespread and persisting deprivation" of federal
rights by the states in such matters. In short, federal judges—not
Congress—would have the authority to determine whether states
had been discriminating against people. If they couldn't, states

would be free to violate people's rights without compensation.

How many instances of illegal discrimination by the states would it take to meet this standard? The ultraconservative right-wing justices on the Supreme Court did not answer this question. They did, however, insist that anecdotal evidence of such deprivations presented at congressional committee hearings was not enough to force compensation. Never mind that these hearings were how Congress had always gathered such evidence against states committing wrongdoings. Never mind, either, the ultra-Right's constant complaint of liberal judges "legislating from the bench." Legislating from the bench is fine, it seems, as long as the action achieves this group's particular goals.

With the addition of these two requirements the Rehnquist Court single-handedly undermined the federal safety net that had been constructed over sixty years to protect individuals from out-of-control state legislatures. In effect, the Court has made it virtually impossible for Congress to hold states (and all their agencies) accountable for violating people's federal rights. And by depriving the people of any effective remedy to vindicate those rights, the Supreme Court elevated the doctrine of states' rights over popular sovereignty. Not only did it undermine decades of history—it clearly undermined the Constitution!

The ADA and Patricia Garrett didn't fare well under these new parameters. In a 2001 5-4 decision written by Chief Justice Rehnquist himself, the Supreme Court bounced Garrett's lawsuit out of court without even deciding whether her state employer had violated the ADA. In fact, Rehnquist never even described what happened to Garrett in the Court's opinion. He deliberately ignored the suffering and trials of Garrett in order to further his hard-line agenda. The crux of Rehnquist's sanitized opinion was that there was insufficient evidence presented to Congress that the fifty states had discriminated against the disabled. Thus, states could not be sued for discriminatory damages.

But let's consider the evidence. Congress had held thirteen hearings on the subject of discrimination against the disabled. In addition, Congress had created a *special task force* to examine the need for comprehensive legislation protecting the rights of disabled Americans. That task force convened hearings in *every* state, which were attended by more than thirty thousand people, including thousands who had experienced discrimination firsthand.

Those thirteen federal hearings included testimony regarding at least *three hundred* instances of discrimination by state governments against disabled people. Examples of such discrimination included:

• Evidence that most of the agencies in one state discriminated against cancer survivors who applied for state jobs for over five years *after* they had been treated for cancer.

• A state school refused to exempt a deaf teacher from complying with a "listening skills" requirement.

• A state refused to hire a blind employee as the director of an agency for the blind, even though he was the most qualified applicant.

• A woman crippled by arthritis was denied a job teaching at a state university because the university didn't want its students to have to look at her.

- A microfilmer who worked at a state department of transportation was fired, he was told, because his supervisors discovered that he had epilepsy.

There are several hundred more examples from these congressional hearings alone. Although these terrible instances occurred all over America, the majority of justices on the Supreme Court didn't think it was sufficient to punish the states for discrimination under the ADA.

This was not the only time that the Rehnquist Court struck down a federal law allowing lawsuits against discriminatory state agencies. For example, in a 1999 decision written by Chief Justice Rehnquist, the Supreme Court ruled that an inventor could not collect damages from a for-profit state agency that had stolen his patented invention, even though the agency was selling it for millions of dollars. Because of this decision, the over five million Americans who have patented their inventions can no longer be compensated if a state agency steals their intellectual property. States can also violate the rights of the more than one hundred million Americans who own copyrighted works like books, plays, music, and movies.

In another 5-4 decision written by Justice O'Connor in 2000, the Court ruled that more than 4.5 million Americans who are employed by state governments cannot recover damages from their employers when they engage in illegal age discrimination.

In case after case decided by the Supreme Court in the last ten years, a bare majority of the Court's five far-right justices have systematically struck down federal laws passed to protect citizen rights of individuals. It has been a persistent onslaught against average people, perpetuated by relentless judicial activism.

The hypocrisy of the radical Right in usurping the rights of Americans is endless. Indeed, one of the most famous and conservative appeals court judges in the entire country, John Noonan Jr., has written an entire book—*Narrowing the Nation's Power: The Supreme Court Sides With the States*—showing how activist the Rehnquist Court's states' rights decisions have become.

First of all, nothing in the text of the Constitution or the writings of the framers supports making it more difficult for states to be held accountable for discrimination. So much for strictly interpreting the Constitution's text and following the intent of the framers. Furthermore, in order to allow states to violate these rights of individuals, the Court has had to strike down laws passed by our elected representatives in Congress—again, the exact definition of judicial activism. Instead, the five conservative justices on the Supreme Court substituted their own policy judgments for the judgments of the Congress and the president. More importantly, this judicial activism—like the case with punitive damages awards—is consistently in favor of states and big business, and at the expense of everyday Americans.

Finally, the Rehnquist Court is making it more difficult for laws to be construed as constitutional—even after the laws are passed. So, retroactively, it is making it harder for federal legislation to pass the increasingly difficult test of ultraconservative legitimacy. Thus, when Congress passed the ADA in 1990, it had no reason to know that the Supreme Court would, seven years later, require detailed congressional findings to allow states to be sued. But the Court is perfectly willing to apply these new constitutional rules to earlier legislation when doing so promotes a conservative agenda. This is especially true in criminal cases. The Rehnquist Court rarely, if ever, allows criminal defendants convicted in state courts to take advantage of new constitutional rules in their favor. Why not? Because doing so would not be fair to state court judges, who could not have foreseen the new rules when the defendants were convicted—and thus could not have been expected to follow them. This is the exact opposite of the Court's standard involving federal courts. Once again, in order to further their ultraconservative agenda, the Court will rule however it sees fit.

In striking down federal laws passed to protect the rights of everyday Americans from unjust state discrimination, the Rehnquist Court has completely refuted the views of the framers and Chief Justice Marshall. Those men believed that a court should strike down a federal law in only the rarest of cases, when the violation of the Constitution was unassailably clear. Instead, the Rehnquist Court has adopted the reverse position that federal laws are presumed to be unconstitutional unless *Congress* can overcome that presumption. To overcome this presumption, Congress is required to satisfy the increasingly difficult demands of the ultraconservative court. The right-wing members of the Court have persistently ignored the overriding principle articulated in the text of the Constitution that sovereignty lies in the people rather than in individual states.

Even worse, the right-wing justices have resurrected the doctrine of states' rights. Until ten years ago, this antiquated doctrine had been consigned to the dustbin of history along with similar doctrines such as "separate but equal." Now, the right-wing justices have elevated this doctrine over the rights of millions of people whose rights are being trampled on by the states. And the states are doing so in direct violation of federal laws passed by the people's elected representatives in Congress.

The right-wing justices on the Supreme Court have reached these decisions without ever examining the facts of the individuals' cases they heard. They never decided whether the states had actually infringed on an inventor's patent; they never reviewed the alleged discrimination against an older worker; they never examined the facts involving discrimination against a recovering breast cancer victim. Instead, they have dismissed these cases and struck down the federal laws allowing compensation based on their own subjective, newly divined standards, which have nothing whatsoever to do with the Constitution's text or history.

But this isn't new. It's another example of just how the radical Right, empowered by a cadre of hard-line justices on the Supreme Court, will say and do anything to advance its agenda. Neither history, federal law, nor the rights of average Americans matter in its quest to remake America in its image.

JUDICIAL ACTIVISM IN OUR TIME

Top Nine Judicial Activist Decisions

By The Rehnquist Court In The Last Ten Years

---

*1. Grat*_z *v. Bollinger,* 539 U.S. 244 (2003). In an opinion written by Chief Justice Rehnquist, five-justice majority rules that University of Michigan's undergraduate affirmative action program is unconstitutional.

2. State Farm Mutual Automobile Insurance Company v. Campbell, 538 U.S. 408 (2003). In an opinion written by Justice Kennedy, six-justice majority rules that punitive damage awards are constitutional only if the ratio of punitive damages to compensatory damages is less than ten to one.

3. Board of Trustees of the University of Alabama v. Garrett, 531 U.S. 356 (2001). In an opinion written by Chief Justice Rehnquist, five-justice majority strikes down provisions of Americans With Disabilities Act permitting disabled state employees who are victims of discrimination to sue their state employers for money damages.

4. Kimel v. Florida Board of Regents, 528 U.S. 62 (2000). In an opinion written by Justice O'Connor, five-justice majority strikes down provisions of Age Discrimination in Employment Act permitting state employees who are victims of age discrimination to sue their state employers for money damages.

5. *United States v. Morrison*, 529 U.S. 598 (2000). In an opinion written by Chief Justice Rehnquist, five-justice majority strikes down provisions of the Violence Against Women Act permitting female victims of spousal abuse to sue their abusers for damages in federal court.

6. *Printz v. United States*, 521 U.S. 898 (1997). In an opinion written by Justice Scalia, five-justice majority strikes down Brady Handgun Violence Prevention Act provisions requiring state and local law enforcement officers to conduct background checks on prospective handgun purchasers.

7. *City of Boerne v. Flores*, 521 U.S. 507 (1997). In an opinion written by Justice Kennedy, six-justice majority strikes down Religious Freedom Restoration Act provisions prohibiting the government from substantially burdening a person's exercise of his or her religion.

8. *Seminole Tribe of Florida v. Florida*, 517 U.S. 44 (1996). In an opinion written by Chief Justice Rehnquist, five-justice majority strikes down provisions of Indian Gaming Regulatory Act permitting Indian tribes to sue a state to enforce the act's requirement that the state negotiate in good faith with respect to a gambling compact between the state and the tribe.

9. *Adarand Constructors, Inc. v. Pena*, 515 U.S. 200 (1995). In an opinion written by Justice O'Connor, five-justice majority strikes down provisions of the Small Business Act requiring that

preferences be given to racial and ethnic minorities who bid on federal government contracts.

My issue here is not with the outcome in any of these cases, but with the ideological inconsistency. How can the Far Right insist there is one "correct" way to reach judicial decisions when their favorite justices shift philosophies at will to reach a desired outcome? How can Scalia and Thomas so clearly divine original intent, then turn around and parse the Commerce Clause on behalf of states' rights and the NRA, then against states' rights and medical marijuana? Have they discovered some "specific ratio" for punitive damages? I haven't a clue.

The truth is that judges must examine each case that comes before them. They must engage in the very human task of resolving the facts under our Constitution—and with many years of legal precedents—as best they can. There is no single rule that encompasses the extraordinary variety of issues put before our courts. The world does not fit into such a neat basket. We can criticize our judges till hell freezes over—but walk a mile in their shoes.

CHAPTER TWENTY-ONE

THE HOLIEST OF HOLIES

The Twenty Biggest Powerbrokers of the Far Right.

1. JAY SEKULOW

As chief counsel for the American Center for Law and Justice (ACLJ), Pat Robertson's fundamentalist Christian answer to the ACLU, Jay Sekulow, forty-nine, is the evangelical extreme's legal point man in D.C.. One of the "Four Horsemen," a powerful group of lobbyists formed to promote ultraconservative candidates to the federal judiciary, Sekulow has presented numerous oral arguments to the Supreme Court. In the landmark 1993 Lambs Chapel case, he helped the Christian fringe win the right to advance their agenda in public schools on free speech grounds. "Our public schools began as ministries of the church," said Sekulow. "Now it is time to return them to the Lord."

Sekulow also directly exerts ideological influence from within the Justice Department itself. He is a member of the faculty of its Office of Legal Education, where he instructs federal prosecutors on many hot-button extreme-right issues. It's not surprising that the *National Law Journal* has twice named Sekulow one of the "100 Most Influential Lawyers" in the United States. Sekulow helped to draft the Defense of Marriage Act, signed into law in 1996, which allows individual states to reject the legitimacy of same-sex marriage licenses granted elsewhere. Sekulow's vehemently parochial agenda reaches millions via massive direct mailings and weekly radio and television broadcasts.

2. JAMES DOBSON

Founder and former head of Focus on the Family, James Dobson built an evangelical empire out of the Colorado Springs ministry he created in 1977. Dobson, a pediatric psychiatrist, dovetailed pop-psychology parenting advice with fundamentalist religious dogma through Focus on the Family's prolific publishing and broadcasting concerns. As his ministry's popularity grew, Dobson's advocacy of spanking children gave way to his obsessive, increasingly virulent condemnation of homosexuality. His ministries maintain that through prayers and counseling, teenagers can be cured of any "pre-homosexuality" symptoms they display.

In 1983 Dobson created the Family Research Council, a lobbying group designed to preach his evangelical message in Washington. From 1985 to 1986 he served on Attorney General Edwin Meese's Commission on Pornography. Though he showed only grudging enthusiasm for George W. Bush's candidacy in 2000, by 2004 Dobson had created yet another offshoot of his ministries—Focus on Family Action—specifically to stump for Bush. Since stepping down as head of Focus on the Family, Dobson continues to keep himself and his radical anti-abortion, anti-gay agenda in the public eye. On *Justice Sunday II*, in August of 2005, he condemned America's judiciary as "unelected, unaccountable, and arrogant," words which describe his lobbying efforts perfectly.

3. TOM DELAY

Arguably Congress's most outspoken member, Tom DeLay,

fifty-eight, has been the House majority leader since 2002. He has recently been embroiled in controversy for his questionable conduct during the Terri Schiavo crisis. "The men responsible will have to answer for their behavior," said DeLay of the judges who ruled not to keep her on life support. This cryptic statement drew much flak in the wake of several high-profile murders of judges and their relatives.

DeLay was an exterminator in Sugar Land, Texas, before running for Congress, a decision he made due to his frustration with federal regulations. He is nicknamed "The Hammer," a reference to his severe tactics in enforcing party discipline. (Not to be confused with his nickname during college, "Hot Tub Tom," because of his reputed way with women.) "I'm aggressive, and I've been aggressive all my life," he has said. His views are among the most conservative in Congress—he regularly attacks modern culture on the floor of Congress by denouncing birth control, the theory of evolution, and day care. He is unafraid to rebut even the White House, as he did when he opposed the Bush administration's low-income tax cuts. "The last time I checked they [the executive branch] don't have a vote." Although DeLay spearheaded the impeachment proceedings against President Clinton, it was revealed that he may have committed perjury himself during a civil lawsuit in 1994.

Recently DeLay has been an outspoken critic of "liberal" federal judges, and has even advocated removing them from office or defunding certain courts. In August of 2005, DeLay spoke on *Justice Sunday II*, assailing activist judges and calling for more conservative appointments to the federal bench.

4. DR. RICHARD LAND

"As director of the political arm of the Southern Baptist Convention, Richard Land has enjoyed a long and close relationship with the born-again Bush," *Time* magazine observed in 2004. That's something of an understatement. Land, fifty-eight, is a two-time Bush appointee to the United States Commission on International Religious Freedom (and he was appointed to a third term in July of 2005). He is widely recognized as one of the most persuasive advisers behind the president's stubborn opposition to federally funded stem-cell research.

As the head of the SBC's For Faith and Family Broadcast Ministry, Dr. Land addresses more than 1.5 million radio listeners a week on fundamentalist issues. He has urged his listeners to boycott the Walt Disney Company because of Disney resorts' "Gay Days" promotions and their policy of providing spousal-rights health insurance to same-sex couples. Dr. Land is rabidly anti-abortion, comparing pro-choice advocates to 1860s anti-abolitionists and accusing liberal lawmakers of protecting endangered wildlife at the expense of unborn children.

5. RICHARD MELLON SCAIFE

The *Washington Post* estimates that in over four decades, Richard Scaife, seventy-three, has contributed $620 million to a galaxy of ultraconservative individuals and organizations. Born into the Mellon fortune, Scaife followed in his mother Sarah's footsteps as a philanthropist. He also inherited her interest in women's rights—the anti-abortion movement is possibly the only radically conservative goal Scaife doesn't back directly. "Our funding," Scaife maintains, "is based on our support of ideas like limited government, individual rights, and a strong defense."

Scaife dollars have substantially underwritten the Heritage Foundation, the Federalist Society, the Free Congress Foundation, the American Enterprise Institute, the Cato Institute, and the Pacific Legal Foundation, to name just a few. Scaife's network of right-wing think tanks, candidates, activists, and attorneys has been active in almost every area of American policymaking. Thanks to Richard Scaife's generosity, the radical Right has fought welfare, affirmative action, and environmental laws and worked to undermine the judiciary and free big business of taxes and regulations for nearly half a century.

Though Richard Scaife maintains a low media profile, he has had several memorable brushes with journalists, especially in the years before he gave up drinking. When a *Nation* reporter approached him for an interview in 1981, he dismissed the woman by calling her a "fucking Communist cunt."

6. TIM GOEGLEIN

Deputy director of the White House's Office of Public Liaison, Tim Goeglein, forty-one, is the religious Right's ambassador to the Oval Office. While in college, the Indiana-bred Goeglein interned for Senator Dan Coates and Vice President Dan Quayle. He became ultraconservative candidate Gary Bauer's spokesman during the 2000 presidential primary race, and when Bauer dropped out, Goeglein joined the Bush campaign. After Bush took office, Karl Rove hired Goeglein to mediate between the White House and the religious Right. "When we call Tim," says the National Association of Evangelicals' Ted Haggard, "his office responds. He's the one evangelical leaders across America have a relationship with."

"It is Goeglein's job," says the *Washington Post*, "to make sure conservatives are happy, in the loop and getting their best ideas before the president and turned into laws." As a devout born-again Christian, Goeglein freely admits that his job is controlled by his faith. "Everything emanates from there," he says. Goeglein has tirelessly worked to sell Christian conservatives on Bush policy and to influence the President on behalf of fundamentalist ministries. Since Bush's re-election, Goeglein has concentrated on facilitating the nomination of Christian activist judges to the federal bench.

7. C. BOYDEN GRAY

An heir to the R.J. Reynolds tobacco fortune, Gray, sixty-two, graduated magna cum laude from Harvard University and earned a law degree from the University of North Carolina Law School. After clerking for Chief Justice Earl Warren, the future leader of the Four Horsemen joined the D.C. firm *Wilmer, Cutler and Pickering*. The *New Republic* stated that Gray, "turns dirty lobbying into activism." *At that firm he successfully helped corporate interests to flaunt, circumvent, and overturn environmental and product safety regulations.* Capitol Hill insiders believe that Gray ghostwrote the industry-friendly Clean Water Act for Bob Dole.

Gray served as chief counsel to George H.W. Bush during his terms as vice president and president and was selected to serve George W. Bush on the Bush-Cheney Transition Advisory Committee for the Department of Justice. He remains an indispensable White House legal strategist. Gray is a board member of the *Federalist Society and Progress for America and* co-chair of Freedom Works, a reincarnation of Citizens for a Sound Economy—all extreme-right organizations. A gifted fundraiser, Gray is able to persuade both old-money Republicans and young neo-conservatives to support the radical Right's assault on the Constitution.

Gray was tapped by Trent Lott to spearhead the Republican fight against filibustering federal judicial nominees. And as head of the Committee For Justice Gray oversaw their infamous ad campaign, which tried to smear Democrats with the tag "Catholics Need Not Apply" during William H. Pryor Jr.'s nomination hearings. Through his manifold connections, Gray personally coordinates with two hundred ultraconservatives on a weekly basis.

8. TIM LAHAYE

Dr. Tim LaHaye is famous as coauthor of the multimillion best-selling *Left Behind* apocalyptic fiction series, a nationally recognized speaker on Bible prophecy, and the founder and president of Tim LaHaye Ministries. As cofounder of the Pre-Trib Research Center, a "think tank" committed to the study, proclamation, teaching, and defending of the pre-tribulation Rapture and related end-time prophecy, LaHaye believes that the sixty-six canonical books of the Old and New Testaments, alone in their entirety, comprise the God-inspired scriptures, which, therefore, are inerrant in their truth and authenticity.

In 1970, LaHaye set up the Institute for Creation Research and co-founded the Moral Majority, and he created the Council for National Policy in 1981, an invitation-only collection of the country's best and most conservative minds. A founder of Christian Heritage College and a contributor to the founding of Patrick Henry College, Dr. LaHaye was also the chairman of Sun Myung Moon's Coalition for Religious Freedom.

In his 2003 nonfiction work *Mind Siege*, coauthored with

David Noebel, Dr. LaHaye outlines his model view of society as one that melds Christian principles with the federal government to produce a "Christian and pro-moral community."

9. ED MEESE

As attorney general under Ronald Reagan from 1985 to 1988, Ed Meese was a forceful proponent of "originalism" and consequently "strict constructionist" judges. He was responsible for the successful nominations of Justice Antonin Scalia and the chief justice nomination of William Rehnquist, as well as the failed bids of Robert Bork and Douglas Ginsburg. He opposed affirmative action and *Miranda* rights and asked the Supreme Court to overturn *Roe v. Wade* and the ban on school prayer.

Meese, seventy-three, has long been an advocate of judicial restraint and an outspoken critic of "activist judges." A member of the Four Horsemen, he brings his extensive political and legal experience to the group in its advocacy of ultraconservative judicial nominees. He is also a broker finding common political interests between business conservatives and right-wing Christians. Meese is a fellow at the Heritage Foundation, where he works to promote conservative judges to the federal judiciary. He strongly believes that our Bill of Rights should not restrict state governments at all in their relationship with American citizens; these protections simply wouldn't apply.

10. MICHAEL FARRIS

Michael Farris is the founder of both the Home School Legal Defense Association (HSLDA) and Patrick Henry College. As a constitutional lawyer he has won cases for home-school and religious rights before the Supreme Court. Farris, fifty-three, has been instrumental in pioneering and Christianizing the home-school movement, and has emphasized the rights of parents to provide a religious education for their children. Farris himself has ten children, all of whom were homeschooled.

Farris, who was ordained as a Baptist minister in 1983, founded Patrick Henry College in order to train a new generation of Christian politicians. Eighty-five percent of its students are homeschooled, and it is tied with Georgetown as the college with the most student interns at the White House. Farris himself has written nine nonfiction books and three novels, all of which warn against "MTV, Internet porn, abortion, homosexuality, greed, and accomplished selfishness."

Patrick Henry College, which maintains strict courtship rituals between men and women, was created using donations from prominent evangelicals, including Tim LaHaye, whose portrait hangs in the school's main hall. Farris hopes it will someday become one of the most respected colleges in America. One day, he says, "an Academy Award winner will walk down the aisle to accept his trophy. On his way, he'll get a cell-phone call; it will be the president, who happens to be his old Patrick Henry roommate, calling to congratulate him."

11. TED HAGGARD

"Pastor Ted," forty-nine, counts thirty million born-again Christians in his flock. As founding father of the 11,000-member New Life Church and head of the 45,000-church National Association of Evangelicals (NAE), he has the ear of fundamentalist Christian activists all over the globe. As a welcome advisor to the Bush White House, Ted Haggard is arguably the most politically influential evangelical next to James Dobson.

With his massive "Evangelical Vatican" megachurch head-quarters in Colorado, enormously successful book and tape series, and regular television appearances, Ted Haggard is an icon of the religious Right's unapologetic media friendliness. Recently Haggard has lost favor in some parts of the fundamentalist community for his specific belief in a somewhat fallible God and for telling an audience of one million Christians that God would force Saddam Hussein to peaceably step down if they all prayed together.

12. RICHARD EPSTEIN

Epstein, sixty-two, is a distinguished legal academic and prolific author of highly opinionated and thoroughly researched books on a variety of legal topics. Since 1972, he has taught law at the University of Chicago. As a television commentator, educator, and editorial writer, Epstein is the button-down, scholarly face of extreme-right activism. A committed libertarian, Richard Epstein is a Cato Institute Scholar and a Federalist Society member. At one time or another, he has been involved with such radical right-wing policy groups as the Independent Institute and the American Friends of the Institute for Economic Affairs.

Epstein is the intellectual godfather of Constitution in Exile, which seeks to return the country to a pre-New Deal America. He maintains that all economic legislation, including zoning and minimum wage laws, should be repealed. Epstein also supports and promotes extreme conservative views on intellectual property, affirmative action, global warming, states' rights, public health care, unrestrained free-market capitalism, and a variety of other issues.

13. TONY PERKINS

Tony Perkins is currently the president of the Family Research Council, an offshoot of Focus on the Family, the ultraconservative lobbying group founded by James Dobson, his close friend. He was the leading force and organizer of *Justice Sunday* and *Justice Sunday II*, watched by millions.

Perkins was a member of the Louisiana House of Representatives from 1996 to 2004. His bid for the U.S. Senate in 2002 failed, in large part due to Perkins's ties to prominent white supremacists. In 1996, as the campaign manager to another Senate hopeful, Perkins paid David Duke—the former Grand Wizard of the Ku Klux Klan—for his mailing list. As a result, the campaign Perkins worked for was fined $3,000 by the Federal Election Commission and further bids for higher office were pragmatically impossible.

Perkins is an outspoken critic of the current federal judiciary and has publicly lobbied for more conservative justices. He has been likened to Ralph Reed, the former head of the Christian Coalition, for his youth, slick demeanor, and ultraconservative politics, a combination which will likely increase his political clout in the future.

14. LEONARD LEO

Credit Horseman Leonard Leo with turning the once unimportant Federalist Society into the formidable force it has become in Washington today. As the society's executive vice president, he now vets all judicial candidates for the White

House—a responsibility previously reserved for the American Bar Association. A graduate of Cornell University Law, Leo clerked for two federal judges and worked as an associate attorney specializing in gaming law and casino regulation before joining the Federalist Society.

As the new head of the Republican National Committee's Catholic Outreach, Leo successfully made ideological bedfellows out of Roman Catholics and Protestant fundamentalists. He publicly urged priests to instruct their parishioners to vote Bush in '04. "I think there's nothing wrong with priests counseling their parishioners [about] certain nonnegotiable issues in the church," Leo said. "As faithful Catholics they need to consider those issues when selecting candidates." His work paid off—religious voters who didn't vote in 2000 flocked to the polls four years later, assuring four more years in the White House for Bush.

15. ROY MOORE

Few judges ever earn the notoriety that Roy Moore has in the last two years. Moore, fifty-eight, was the chief justice of the

Alabama Supreme Court until November 14, 2003, when the other eight members of his court unanimously voted to remove him from office. They did so because Moore had blatantly and unapologetically violated a federal court ruling to remove copies of the Ten Commandments from his courtroom. Even after a federal district court ruled he had to remove the Ten Commandments monument, Moore refused. "There is no morality without God," he said, and further maintained that the Ten Commandments in particular form the moral basis for U.S. law.

Since being removed from office, Moore has considered a further political career. It is likely Moore will run for either the Senate or the governorship of Alabama in the future. His popularity in the state has improved enormously since the Ten Commandments incident, of which he says he has "no regrets."

16. MICHAEL GERSON

To prepare to write George W. Bush's acceptance speech for the Republican nomination in 2000, Michael Gerson read every acceptance speech every major presidential candidate had given since 1960. He knew the world would be watching the Texan governor and, more importantly, judging what came out of his mouth. Now Bush's chief speechwriter, Gerson, forty, shares both the spiritual and political worldview of the man who speaks his words. A fellow born-again Christian, Gerson believes religion has an important place in public affairs. "The danger for America," he says, "is not theocracy".

"Scrubbing public discourse of religious ideas," Gerson has said, "would remove one of the main sources of social justice in our history."

Gerson studied theology at Wheaton College and later worked for Prison Fellow Ministries. His religious convictions color the language he uses, and he does not shy away from advocating religion in public life. Gerson is one reason for Bush's overtly religious addresses—including the speech on how the United States had to "rid the world of evil."

Gerson is a policy advisor and sits in on the morning staff meeting with top White House aides. Gerson's full-time staff of writers, fact-checkers, and researchers crafts the language the president will use at his average of three speaking engagements per day. When Bush said, in his 2005 State of the Union address, "Judges have a duty to faithfully interpret the law, not legislate from the bench," Gerson was the man behind the speech.

17. BILL FRIST

As the Senate majority leader, Bill Frist is the third most powerful Republican in the country. Before running for political office, Frist was a cardiothoracic surgeon. Frist is widely considered a presidential contender for the 2008 election; he has stated publicly that he will not run for senatorial re-election in 2006. Although he appeared at the first *Justice Sunday* broadcast in April 2005, he was not invited to *Justice Sunday II* because of his change in position on the issue of stem-cell research. Although he had sided with the Bush administration in restricting the research to existing stem-cell lines, on July 29, 2005, he publicly reversed this position, advocating expanding the research to include other embryos as well. Frist has also been active in the battle to promote conservative judges, though he lost political capital with the Senate's filibuster compromise in May of 2005.

18. DAVID BARTON

David Barton, fifty-one, is the vice chairman of the Texas Republican Party, and perhaps is best known on Capitol Hill for his religious-oriented tours of the Capitol. Barton's for-profit, Texas-based advocacy organization, WallBuilders, claims that America was a Christian nation at the time of its founding. It also asserts that any separation of church and state is a lie perpetrated by Supreme Court justices in the twentieth century.

Barton's numerous books and videotapes—among them *The Myth of Separation*—are wildly popular in the evangelical Christian community, though not respected by historians.. He is close friends with numerous Republican politicians, including Tom DeLay, whom he advised on the Pledge Patriot Act—meant to keep the phrase "under God" in the Pledge of Allegiance.

19. GROVER NORQUIST

"I don't want to abolish government," says Grover Norquist, "I simply want to reduce it to the size where I can drag it into the bathroom and drown it in the bathtub." Norquist, forty-eight, is the president of Americans for Tax Reform, and is particularly outspoken against taxation—he has publicly compared the estate tax to the Holocaust.

Although Norquist is best known for his fiscal conservatism, he was originally attracted to the Republican Party because of its staunch anti-Communist stance during the cold war. When he was eleven he read literature by Whittaker Chambers and J. Edgar Hoover that influenced his later views—ironic, given his purported reverence for Vladimir Lenin. (He is said to have a portrait of the revolutionary on his living room wall.)

Norquist is now involved in a variety of ultraconservative causes, and his influence in policy is not limited to fiscal conservatism. He is on the board of the National Rifle Association and the American Conservative Union and has advised California governor Arnold Schwarzenegger on a number of policy issues.

Norquist recognizes the importance of the federal judiciary in upholding ultraconservative legislation.

20. DR. D. JAMES KENNEDY

A former dance instructor with impressive theological credentials, Kennedy, seventy-five, is a luminary of the radical, fundamentalist Right. Kennedy took over as pastor of Fort Lauderdale's Coral Ridge Presbyterian Church in 1959. In 1974 his ministry began airing *The Coral Ridge Hour*, a Sunday-morning evangelical church broadcast now carried on over five hundred television stations. In order to promote "biblical virtues-based culture," Kennedy created the Center for Reclaiming America under the leadership of anti-abortion activist Janet Folger. The CRA spawned a political arm, the Washington, D.C., based Center for Christian Statesmanship. Together, the two groups fundraise, proselytize, and lobby against legal abortion, public education, and especially gay rights.

Kennedy's religious rhetoric is often inflammatory to the point of caricature. He regularly threatens a nationwide

Christian revolution, telling the faithful, "Our job is to reclaim America for Christ, *whatever the cost*." Much of Kennedy's dogma smacks of Reconstructionism—a particularly medieval form of fundamentalism advocating an Old and New Testament theocracy instead of a constitutional government.

And as "Honorable" Mentions . . .
Those who paved the way.

PAT ROBERTSON

Marion Gordon Robertson, also known as Pat, is perhaps the most famous and influential televangelist for the religious Right. Founder of the Christian Coalition, the American Center for Law and Justice, and the Christian Broadcasting Network, Robertson is single-handedly responsible for the increase of political power of the religious Right in the 1980s and 1990s. Since he left the Christian Coalition in 2001, however, it has lost much of its membership and clout. Despite this, Robertson, who is seventy-five years old, continues to lobby for conservative political causes, and recently has spoken out about the federal judiciary. On August 2, 2005, Robertson prayed on television for more vacancies on the Supreme Court, encouraging others to do so as well.

PHYLLIS SCHLAFLY

Since helping defeat the Equal Rights Amendment in the 1970s, Phyllis Schlafly, eighty-one, has continued as president of the Eagle Forum, which she founded in 1972. The Eagle Forum is a conservative advocacy group that focuses mainly on

women's issues. Schlafly recently testified in Congress in favor
of the Federal Marriage Amendment, which would ban same-sex
marriage. She also appeared on Justice Sunday II.

ORRIN HATCH

A five-time U.S. senator from Utah, Hatch is outspoken in his
religious, ultraconservative beliefs, though unlike many politicians
on the religious Right, he is a Mormon. After a failed presidential
bid in 2000, Hatch, seventy-one, continued to chair the Judiciary
Committee until 2004, when he was replaced by Arlen Specter.
He has continued to push for conservative policies in the Senate,
though his views—including his advocacy of stem-cell research—
are less conservative than those of many of his colleagues.

JERRY FALWELL

One of the most well-known televangelists in America, Falwell
founded the Faith and Values Coalition in 2004, a resurrection of
his earlier lobbying group, the Moral Majority, which dissolved
in 1989. The Faith and Values Coalition was formed to promote
conservative religious views in U.S. policymaking. Most famous
for his outrageous public statements, Falwell, seventy-two, has
received a volley of criticism since September 11, 2001, both for
his assertion that homosexuals were responsible for the terrorist
attacks and for his claim that Muhammad, the religious figurehead
of Islam, was a terrorist.

CHAPTER TWENTY-TWO

WHAT I KNOW

I am anticipating the grenades that will likely be tossed at me by the right-wing groups mentioned herein when this book hits the stands. I can hear it now: "She's one of those liberal, atheistic, America-hating, queer-loving media types that are out to subvert religion in this country." Sigh. Then again, maybe they will consider my words unworthy of their response. That gives me a momentary wave of relief. Isn't it sad that we're living in a time where, if someone speaks out, they literally have to duck and cover? At the risk of sounding like a "victim," I've started to contemplate the almost certain backlash: tax audits, pressure on Court TV, or even worse.

This is not the country I was born into. It is certainly not the country I pledged to defend when I took solemn oaths, first as an attorney, then as a Republican judge. But then, I'm a Texan. The last thing I can contemplate is sitting quietly as some group pulls the political wool over my eyes. Yet there are moments, you know them, when one says to oneself, "Just shut up and go home. Tomorrow is another day."

But I cannot and will not do that. I love my country too much. I no longer believe things will get better, unless and until America's real majority—the rational, pragmatic, tolerant,

Constitution-loving preponderance of U.S. citizens—expresses its outrage and takes action against this attempted hijacking of our beloved Republic.

Throughout history, the vast majority of the nation's judges have served this country well. Yes, there have been some bad rulings, philosophical disagreements, and even political concessions over the years, but all in all, the American judiciary has been the institution that our founders envisioned. Its diversity and independence have kept us essentially on course; sometimes we stray a bit too far to the left or right, but for the most part, we move strongly in the (uh) right direction. Make that the "correct" direction.

However, today the majority of American citizens have voluntarily abdicated their influence at all levels of public life, from the school boards to the Supreme Court, so that an enormous vacuum has been created. The radical Right has had virtually no resistance as it fills this void, attempting to capture all three branches of the federal government. Contrary to its self-professed image as a maligned "people of faith" and oppressed minority, this powerful group has tremendous sway over the country. The industry of religion, composed primarily of born-again, fundamentalist sects, is staggering—television, radio, books, megachurches—and its influence on politics and policy is growing exponentially.

I have no quarrel with any person's religious or political values, but I will fight to my dying day for the moral and just, but yes, secular government our framers willed to each of us. I just pray that the silent majority that I believe exists will rise up to defend our precious liberties—and the glorious nation we still inhabit.

ACKNOWLEDGMENTS

I'd like to thank some terrific researchers for their work on this: Lauren Sasser, Bruce Bennett, Joe DiMento, Catherine Fryszczyn and Monica Jasty. I have mixed emotions about my ultimate task master, Web Stone (just kidding) who was relentless in his drive to see this book out in time to respond to the Supreme Court debate now underway. His partner, Shawn Coyne, has been invaluable, as has Rugged Land publicist Zoe Feigenbaum; and of course my angel, publicist extraordinaire, Heidi Krupp. Very special thanks to my wonderful bosses at Court TV, especially Henry Schlieff and Art Bell, who fervently believe in the right to free speech—no matter the consequences, and my wonderful program staff headed by Shawn Giangeruso. I grovel at the feet of my true boss, Barbara Stansell, who runs my life completely and the man I love beyond words my soul mate, Jim Logan.